**Anatomy
of the
Ship**

The Schooner
Bertha L.
Downs

**Anatomy
of the
Ship**

The Schooner

Bertha L. Downs

Basil Greenhill & Sam Manning

Naval
Institute
Press

This book is dedicated
with our undying regard
to Captain W J Lewis Parker,
United States Coast Guard, retired —
scholar, gentleman, and friend.

FRONTISPIECE

The *Bertha L. Downs* of New Haven,
Connecticut, deep laden. Although she has
weigh on her there appears to be little or
no wind. The vessel appears to have been
on the starboard tack and to have rolled a
little starboard in the slight swell, bringing
the booms over and the topsails up against
the jumpstay and the peak halliards.
(*W J Lewis Parker collection*)

© Basil Greenhill and Sam Manning 1995

First published in Great Britain in 1995 by
Conway Maritime Press,
an imprint of Brassey's (UK) Ltd,
33 John Street,
London WC1N 2AT

Published and distributed in the United States of
America and Canada by the Naval Institute Press,
118 Maryland Avenue, Annapolis, Maryland 21402-5035

Library of Congress Catalog Card No. 94-69765

ISBN 1-55750-790-2

Manufactured in Great Britain

Contents

Foreword

This is the first volume in *Conway's Anatomy of the Ship* series to have as its subject a twentieth-century merchant sailing vessel. Numerous photographs are available of the particular vessel herself and of her contemporaries. Moreover, the vessel concerned is representative of a class of sail-propelled tonnage which developed at the very end of the history of the merchant sailing ship and, indeed, came to its greatest development after the sailing vessel had at long last been finally rendered obsolete by the triple expansion engined steamship at the beginning of the 1880s.

For these reasons this volume is somewhat different in structure from its predecessors. In a longer text we have sought to place the vessel in her context against the history of her times, as well as giving her own history in some detail. We have also chosen forty photographs to illustrate the vessel and her contemporaries and to complement the detailed drawings of her structure and fittings.

It may be asked, why this particular vessel, given that the type is of historical interest for the reasons given above? There are several reasons. She was a particularly good example of her class of tonnage. She is of international interest. She was built in the State of Maine, USA, and owned in Connecticut; she became Danish after a transatlantic passage, then Åland Finnish with a strong British shareholding, trading regularly into London River. Finally, she was registered at an Estonian port during Estonia's brief period of freedom between the wars. She was owned by an Estonian/Danish syndicate and became a unit of a fleet of big American-built wooden four-masted schooners operating in the timber trade in the Baltic and to London. These vessels were a phenomenon of the very last days of the sailing vessels in northern Europe, a phenomenon which came to an end only with the Second World War.

We have received help in the preparation of this book from very many people. We would particularly like to thank Captain Francis E Bowker, a veteran with many years at sea in the big schooners; the late Charles Morgan who studied them in depth for a lifetime; the late Captain Karl Victor Karlsson, who was Master of the *Atlas*, ex *Bertha L. Downs* when she was trading to London; Mr Malcolm Appleby, grandson of the *Atlas'* London owner; and Captain Karl Kåhre, who, with the late Edgar Erikson, drew our attention to the interest of the vessel and her later history. Captain Søren Thirslund's help with the detective work necessary to unravel the mystery of her later years has been of the greatest value and he has helped and encouraged us in other ways. Our greatest debt is to Captain W J Lewis Parker, United States Coast Guard, retired, himself a veteran of the Nova Scotian three-master *T.K. Bentley*. Lew Parker is the historian of the big East Coast schooner. His scholarship is profound and rigorous, his research base without parallel. His help and his friendship, unstintingly given, have made possible the recording of the story of the *Bertha L. Downs*.

BASIL GREENHILL
SAM MANNING

Introduction

One day, way back in July 1937, I was returning to Britain from the Baltic, to which I had sailed in the Finnish four-masted barque *Viking* from a west coast British port towards Kotka in the Gulf of Finland. Passing through Copenhagen I took a couple of days out to see a little of that lovely city and especially to walk down to the harbourside. The water in those days was still thronged with small merchant sailing vessels of various kinds. There was Europe's last real brig — she was, in fact, a snow — the *Tjalfe*, used at that time as the headquarters of a yacht club, and there were dozens of schooners and ketches, almost all of them already fitted with auxiliary motors but still looking as handsome as ever, with their round bowed, flat sterned, Danish hulls. At that time vessels of this kind were still being built in Denmark of wood and in relatively large numbers.

As I walked down towards the mouth of Copenhagen harbour and the waters of The Sound I was fascinated to see in the distance eight towering masts each crowned with a tall, thin, tapering topmast, and evidently belonging to sailing vessels considerably bigger than anything I had yet seen. When I reached the dock in which they lay I found that the masts belonged to two four-masted wooden schooners, the *Gunn* and the *Atlas*. They were discharging timber which, I learned, came from the Gulf of Bothnia in the north of the Baltic Sea. Both the schooners were registered as of the port of Pärnu in Estonia. Both, from their very different characteristics, were obviously built in North America, but nevertheless they presented a great contrast one to another.

The *Gunn* was heavily built, straight stemmed, with little sheer. She had a forecastle built out to the sides of the vessel and a short poop similarly constructed. Although built of wood she looked from a distance like a steel ship. She was clearly a west coast built vessel and when I could check on her I found that she had been launched by the Cholberg shipyard in Victoria, British Columbia, Canada, in 1919 for Norwegian owners — as her name suggests. She looked what she was, practical but not handsome, built for a short but profitable working life.

The other schooner, the *Atlas*, was of a different breed altogether. She was flush decked with a strong sheer sweeping upwards to the bows, a curved stem with a bowsprit and a long jibboom with martingale. She had a big deck house forecastle with the foremast coming up through it and a low poop margined with a heavy wooden rail on massive turned stanchions. The after house was half buried in the poop. Her four tall masts, with their topmasts, perfectly balanced the lovely hull. Everything about her suggested a thoroughbred, built in the state of Maine in New England. This indeed she proved to be. She had been launched as the *Bertha L. Downs* at Bath on the Kennebec River in Maine in 1908, but she looked in such magnificent order that she might have been built only a few years before I saw her.

Both vessels, in fact, had clearly been very well kept up and contrasted very favourably with some of the rather run down motor schooners I had seen earlier in my travels in the Baltic. I scarcely realised it at the time, but I was immensely privileged to see the *Atlas*, among the finest and best maintained of the few New England built four-masted schooners surviving anywhere in full working commission in the late 1930s.

The history of the schooner

The easiest way to present a sail to the wind is square, that is, suspended from a spar to which the sail is attached at its top edge and which is slung on the foreside of a mast, around which it can swing to about 45 degrees to the fore and aft line of the vessel on either side. In the days of hand looms it was very difficult to manufacture heavy, strong fabric in pieces of any size, or close woven fabric at all, and sails, therefore, in the days before power looms, were made up of slack woven small pieces of fabric, sewn together. With such material, and with the relatively poor ropes available, only square sails could be made to set reasonably well and so, although it required a lot of gear and manpower to set and handle a big square sail, square sails were the order of the day for larger vessels throughout antiquity and through medieval times.

Somewhere in the shadows of the late 1300s and the early 1400s the three-masted sailing ship, each mast equipped with one or more square sails, developed from the medieval types of vessel, the hulc, the cog, and the early skeleton constructed ships, all of which had been equipped with a single mast on which was set a single square sail. These ships were very bad performers to windward, but the three-masted, square rigged ship, skilfully handled, could perform reasonably well on the wind and so, as a result of her development as what has been called 'the space capsule of the Renaissance', there was a great outburst of exploring and seafaring activity in the late 1400s and the 1500s which was to have enormous implications for the future of western man. In forty years, knowledge of the world beyond Europe was steadily increased until the world was encompassed. The three-masted, square rigged sailing ship in her various forms was to become the standard ocean carrier and the standard warship until the application of compound and triple expansion steam engines to the screw-driven steamship in the 1870s and early 1880s.

The schooner rig was the only complete innovation in the history of the sailing ship after the development of the three-masted, square rigged ship in the fifteenth century. She was the result of development from two entirely different sources into two main types of sailing ship both described as schooners, closely resembling one another in general form of rig and, in later years, influencing one another, yet still revealing their different ancestry. These two types were the 'topsail schooner', the vessel setting square sails from yards on her foretopmast, and so overwhelmingly preponderant in British waters that she was referred to by people in the merchant shipping industry simply as the 'schooner' without the technical qualification 'topsail'; and the fore and aft schooner, without any square canvas (and often, in its smaller versions, without even the foretopmast), which was so dominant in North America that there, in her turn, she was thought of simply as the natural form of schooner, without qualification.

The topsail schooner is thought to have developed from the small two-masted, square rigged ship and to have completed her development by the middle of the eighteenth century. At the same time a sail plan which was to have descendants in common with the topsail schooner existed as its contemporary at sea. There is a clear representation of a small schooner without square topsails dated as early as 1628 in a line engraving by D van Bremden representing Piet Hein's capture of the Plate Fleet off Havana in that year. Vessels of this type probably existed in the late 1500s. These small schooners without square topsails appear to have developed from open boats with two masts, both gaff rigged, with the foremast the shorter of the two and stepped in the eyes of the vessel and the mainmast stepped about amidships. From this type of vessel the schooner without square topsails — the fore and aft schooner — was to develop and there was to be a great deal of cross-fertilisation between the two types of schooner as the years went by.

The development of the schooner appears to have gone hand in hand with the development of sailmaking techniques, with the techniques used in rope making, and with the gradual improvement of the quality of the ironwork used in rigging. The technology of the seventeenth and eighteenth centuries limited the size of the fore and aft rigged vessel. Neither the rope, nor the iron fittings, nor the simple mechanical aids such as blocks, were good enough to stay a tall single stick mast, or to set and control a big gaff sail, even if it had been possible to make a well setting sail with the fabrics and techniques available. These technical limitations held the fore and aft sail, and the schooner rig, in a state of delicate balance. Although unhandy in big seas and on long runs downwind, schooners with their gaff sails were cheaper to build, maintain and man, handier, and more efficient to windward than small vessels with square sails; but as soon as the small fore and aft schooner reached a certain size

the necessary additional canvas had to be square, because to a relatively primitive technology the making and setting of big square sails was a much easier problem than that presented by the gaff sail. Professor E P Morris of Yale University in Connecticut put the problem very well in a book called *The Fore and Aft Rig in America* published by the Yale University Press as long ago as 1927, but now available in a modern reprint. He put it, and it has never been put better, that

> . . . the fore and aft rig was carried over from boats to larger and larger vessels, until the size was reached, varying with the period, on which square sails were superior, there the encroachment came to an end.

There were very good reasons why the schooner of both kinds developed more quickly in North America than in Britain and Europe. They included lack of capital to invest in expensive square rigged vessels; lack of manpower, because labour was more expensive than in Britain; and the fact that schooners required much less work to be done aloft than did square rigged vessels — and work aloft was difficult or impossible in the New England and Eastern Canadian winters. We know from the evidence of contemporary illustrations that by the second half of the eighteenth century schooners were outnumbering all other types of small vessel on the coasts of Maine and Nova Scotia.[1] The development and widespread adoption of the schooner in the United States and British North America was fostered by the Revolution, the Napoleonic Wars and the War of 1812 because by then technology had reached the point at which it was possible to rig a schooner in such a way that when sailing to windward she was able to outdistance square rigged pursuers often much larger than herself. That very distinguished American historian of the ship, the late Howard I Chapelle, recorded the view that 'by the time of the Revolution the schooner was in such general use as to be the most numerous of all classes of carrier', and he went on to say that during the long, unsettled period in the last decade of the eighteenth century and the first two decades of the nineteenth, schooners carried the bulk of cargoes carried in American vessels, and that in August 1814 it was estimated that 9/10ths of the foreign trade of the United States was carried on in schooners.[2]

The developed schooner came back to Britain from North America and the evidence suggests that she began to come back in small numbers in the late eighteenth and early ninteenth centuries through ports in Britain with strong North American trading connections.[3] It is possible that one of the factors in the gradual widespread adoption of the schooner rig for smaller merchant vessels in Britain in the mid nineteenth century was the development in the first half of that century of a great shipbuilding industry in Prince Edward Island in Canada. This industry was financed at first largely from Britain and initially was dependent on skilled immigrants from Britain. The industry specialised in the production of small vessels built to sell on the British market, many of which were rigged as schooners. The use of the schooner rig for small merchant sailing vessels became gradually more and more common in Britain as the century progressed. With the widespread adoption of the three-masted schooner with square topsails on the foretopmast, which began in the 1870s, the

8

British merchant schooner became a bigger vessel, though still rarely more than 100ft long.[4] From 1870 until the First World War, in the last phase of the sailing economy, the schooner and her variant, the ketch, were the predominant type of small British merchant sailing vessels, both in deep water, that is in the Baltic, Mediterranean, Newfoundland and South American trades, and in the home trade about the coasts of the British Isles and Northern Europe.[5]

The use of the ketch rig became more and more common in British waters after 1870 for smaller sailing vessels. The ketch was, if you like, a schooner with her masts reversed, so that the bulk of her canvas was on the fore. It is interesting to speculate why the most common small merchant sailing vessel in North American waters became, by the later nineteenth century, the schooner with a long mainboom and, probably, no foretopmast, while her British equivalent was the ketch. One possible answer is that the weather on the East Coast of North America is, perhaps, on the whole less inclement than that around the British Isles. In British waters, the long boom projecting over the stern and the huge mainsail of many American schooners would often have been extremely difficult to handle. The all inboard rig of the ketch was far easier to handle in really bad weather. On the other hand the probable origin of the ketch in late nineteenth-century Britain as a lengthened smack with a mizzen added must also be borne in mind.[6] So strong did the ketch tradition become in Britain that small schooners and even small brigantines were converted into ketches and at least one United States-built small schooner, the *Empire*, of Bideford, built in New England in 1854, there is no record in Britain of where, was re-rigged as a ketch when she was acquired by Appledore owners in 1886.[7]

It is of interest that even in New England the virtues of the ketch with her all inboard rig as opposed to that of the schooner — at least the fishing schooners which, with their large crews available to handle the sails, tended, until the development of the 'knockabout' schooner in the early twentieth century, to have even longer mainbooms than small merchant schooners — were, somewhat belatedly, considered. Bunting has a reference to a presentation by Professor George Owen at the New York Society of Naval Architects and Marine Engineers in 1945 which appears to have touched on this subject.[8] But this book deals with merchant vessels. The fishing schooner has her own voluminous literature.[9]

In the twentieth century the general development of the economy in Britain, which meant that there was much less work for small sailing vessels on deep water, brought about her decline, and after the First World War no more schooners or ketches were built. In the home trade as the surviving vessels very gradually dropped out of use they were not replaced, principally because of the competition provided by the development of efficient road transport. The last vessels of this type to operate in British waters, the three-masted motor schooner *Kathleen & May*, built at Connah's Quay in 1900 and the motor-ketch *Irene*, built at Bridgwater in 1908, carried their last cargoes in 1960. At the time of writing both survive, the *Kathleen & May* as a museum ship in London and the *Irene* as a cruise vessel.

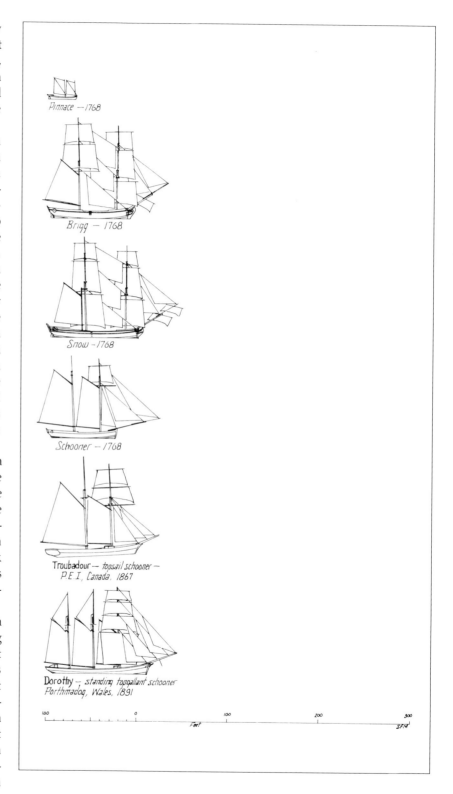

The emergence of the schooner rig in Europe 1768–1891 (scale 1 inch = 100 feet)

The development of the schooner in North America

It is a commonplace of merchant sailing ship history that the big multi-masted schooner was developed on the East and West coasts of North America in the second half of the last century. Few aspects of merchant shipping history have been more thoroughly studied than the story of the big schooners of the East Coast. Captain W J Lewis Parker's exhaustive researches cover the big schooners from their origins — both as a type and as individual vessels — to their social, economic, legal and historical background in New England; the provision of finance, building, management, cargo handling, voyage patterns, and profitability, through to the statistics of length of life and the circumstances of loss or sale to foreign flags.[10]

To recap briefly: in the shadows of the late 1500s the schooner began as a small two-masted vessel. For technical reasons she developed very slowly and by the second half of the 1700s had reached a critical size of about 70ft overall. For economic, political and perhaps even climatic reasons, the schooner developed especially in North America from where the type was reintroduced into increasing use in Britain and Europe in the early 1800s. Three-masted schooners came into existence in the late 1700s. Two of the earliest, the *Jenny* and the *Dispatch*, the latter built in Prince Edward Island, Canada, by the Bristol-based Cambridge family, were registered as of the port of Bristol. But the three-master did not become common until the American Civil War, after which, with the growing demand for the bulk transport of coal from Virginian ports for rapidly developing industrial New England, they became increasingly popular. As trade and the economic size of cargoes increased, so did the schooners grow in size and by the 1870s three-masters were built which could carry 800 tons of coal. The first four-master was launched on the East Coast in 1880, the first East Coast five-master, the *Gov. Ames* at Waldoboro, Maine, in 1888, and what is usually, though not correctly, claimed as the world's first six-masted schooner the *George W. Wells*, 2970 tons gross, 319.3ft long, at Camden, Maine, in 1900. The big American schooners were almost all built of wood. The largest six-master, the *Wyoming*, launched in 1909, was one of the two largest wooden merchant sailing vessels ever constructed. The *Wyoming* measured 329.5ft overall by 50.1ft in the beam and compared closely in size with the six-masted, schooner rigged, iron screw steamship *The Great Britain* of 1844, the first six-masted vessel ever to be registered as a schooner, now restored and open to public view in the old harbour at Bristol in England. She measured 322ft overall with an overall breadth of 50.5ft.

These big schooners were made possible by a number of factors. One was the ready availability of cheap, big timber, in the stands of New England and the old plantations on the seaboard of the Southern States, later supplemented by big timber, especially for masts, carried right across the continent on flat railway cars from the forests of Washington and Oregon States and sometimes delivered by way of a branch line along the street right into the shipyard where the schooner was being built. Other factors were the ready availability of iron wire for standing rigging, and of iron in a form suitable to make diagonal strengthening straps for the hulls, of close woven cotton canvas of heavy gauge for the

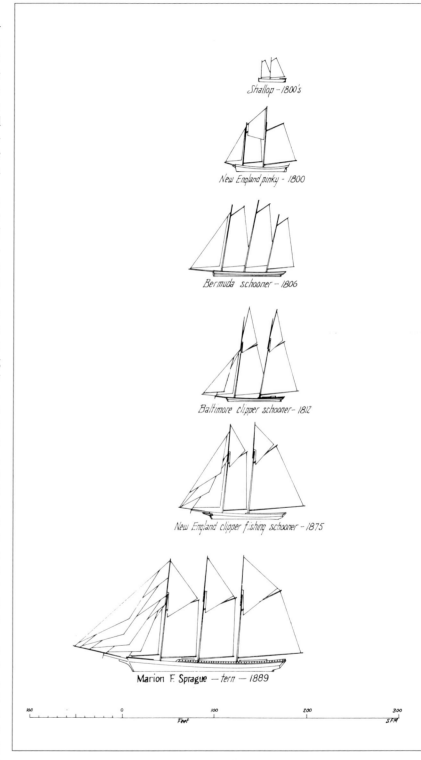

Development of the schooner rig in America 1800–1889 (scale 1 inch = 100 feet)

huge sails, and of high quality rope for running rigging. But the biggest single factor in their development was the steam donkey engine, without which the big schooner could never have existed. Without the steam hoister it would have taken a very big crew at least a day to set the huge gaff sails of the biggest schooners, if indeed they could ever have been set at all. As it was the vessels could operate on a ratio of little more than one ordinary seaman per mast.

Steam was kept up all the time. The huge gaff sails were set by steam, the gaff topsails were sheeted home by steam, the jibs were hoisted by steam. Steam was also used to raise the anchors and in at least some vessels the steam pumps were going all the time because these huge wooden schooners, like almost all wooden vessels, leaked perpetually and because of their size the volume of water which had to be pumped out was proportionately greater than for a small vessel. In the words of Captain Karl V Karlsson, an Ålander who sailed as seaman on the four-master *Edward H. Cole* and later commanded two American-built schooners under the Finnish flag, 'You rang a bell and the winch started turning'. It was this facility which enabled the big schooner to operate with only three or four skilled people and five or six ordinary seamen to handle her. A barque of the same cargo capacity needed two or three times the crew. The *Edward H. Cole*, 1791 tons gross had a crew of eight, the full rigged ship *A.J. Fuller*, 1848 tons gross needed twenty-one men. A steamer of the same cargo capacity needed even more. And these men had to be mostly skilled able seamen, engineers or firemen. The essentials for handling a middle sized four-masted schooner were a first-class master and a mate and a donkeyman of similar calibre; the rest could be ordinary seamen. No wonder that Danish seamen dubbed the large American vessels which came into their waters as 'steam schooners'.

The big wooden schooner was probably at her best as a handy four-master of from 750 tons to 1000 tons gross. In this form and operating in the trades for which she was developed, she may well have been the most efficient type of merchant sailing vessel ever built. But, though some of the later vessels were the only wooden merchant sailing ships ever built in relatively highly capitalised and well mechanised yards, they were still essentially the products of deeply traditional ideas. They had developed slowly, and apart from the iron wire standing rigging they were built according to a long established practice from natural materials which had been in use for many centuries and which were thoroughly understood. They had grown from the two-masted schooner and retained her system of staying, simply extended fore and aft as more and more masts were added.

They had their weaknesses, which were discovered empirically, and they were on the whole short-lived vessels. The forty-five five-masters built on the East Coast between 1888 and 1908 inclusive had an average life of only twelve years. The great *Wyoming* herself was posted missing at sea with all her people in 1921 when she was only thirteen years old. The trouble arose partly from the wooden construction of these very large vessels. But there were difficulties with the rigging. The *Gov. Ames* (the abbreviation in her registered name was designed to reduce the cost of telegraphic communication) the first East Coast five-master, was dis-

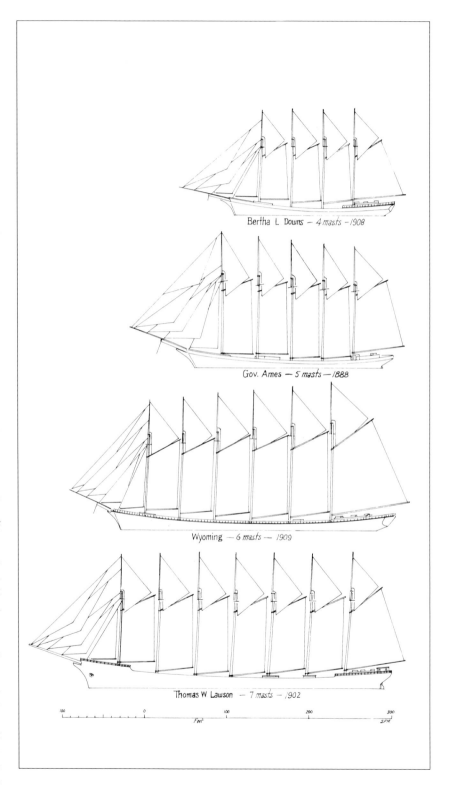

American multi-masted schooners of the late nineteenth and early twentieth centuries

masted on her maiden voyage. R B Forbes, a distinguished American shipowner and merchant, whose working life covered the rise of the multi-masted schooner, wrote of her:

> I have been trying for about 20 years to convince the builders and owners that my stay sail rig is much safer and more manageable than the usual gaff rig. I speak now of the very large schooners, with from 3 to 5 masts. The most prominent objections are, that it is difficult to procure perfectly sound masts of over 28 inches in diameter; it is very unsafe even when the sticks are of good quality to secure them perfectly. All the masts hang or depend on the integrity of the bobstay, the fore stay and the spring stays when run from mast head to mast head; if the bobstays give way when the vessel is pitching into a head sea, the fore mast goes and all the others fall, as a matter of course. In the present rig in order to get canvas enough, the top masts are generally very long and very heavy; the after mast is invariably the longest and is generally so far from the stern that the mizzen or spanker is the largest and most unwieldy sail when it should be the smallest. In squally weather this sail when lowered in gybing sweeps the whole after deck where the steering gear is placed, and greatly encumbers the wheel unless that is protected by a strongly built house; this is a fact so well recognised that the mizzen or after sail is generally the first of the large ones taken in.
>
> If we must have gaff rig the after mast should be nearer the taffrail than usual, and the sail should be fitted to brail in on the gaff to the mast, but it should be so fitted as to be lowered entirely to the deck at times; this arrangement leaves the much smaller gaff and boom to be cared for. The question comes up as to how the after mast is to be stayed. I answer, by staying it by 2 stays, one going to the main rail on each side on an angle about equal to that of the shrouds. It may be said by objectors to this that the boom of the next mast forward of the after mast may interfere with the stays so placed; to this I answer that the stays do not interfere when close hauled and by slightly topping the boom they are not in the way going free.
>
> Now as to the masts hanging together depending on the bob stays, the forestay and on the mast head stays, they must be larger in diameter and consequently more expensive than would be necessary in my stay sail rig where the masts are supported in a fore-and-aft direction like the masts of a ship.[11]

R B Forbes was perfectly right in explaining the weakness of a rigging system entirely dependent in the last resort on the forestays and bobstay. Although he did not know the details, the *Gov. Ames* was already a casualty at the time. In the words of Captain Lewis Parker:

> Two days later she struck a hard gale 50 miles south east of Cape Cod. The stretch which developed in her new rigging gave concern, so she was anchored and her sails furled. The violent pitching which ensued caused a splice to fail in one of her headstays. Almost immediately her foremast and mainmast snapped close to the deck and crashed overboard to starboard, followed in short order by the three after masts which fell fore and aft along the deck. To make matters worse, the helpless hulk dragged and drifted into dangerous proximity to the shoals on Georges Bank before she found holding ground in twenty fathoms of water.[12]

A second weakness is referred to by almost everybody who had experience in sailing big schooners. It was essential to keep the gaff and boom sails small, which meant increasing the number of masts, otherwise the weight of the huge booms, gaffs, and sails working in a seaway caused frequent minor damage. On an ocean voyage the crew of a vessel with big gaff sails had endless work taking in and resetting them to avoid expensive wear in adverse conditions of wind and sea. Moreover, an American writer, Stanley Gerr, has examined the further destructive effects on the fabric of the vessel of the working of the gaffs and booms on an ocean passage and has suggested that,

> with 60 foot, 70 foot and 80 foot spanker booms and 30 foot to 35 foot booms on the other masts, as well as three or four long gaffs, all gyrating with great force about their points of contact with the masts, it is clear that a considerable amount of energy is involved . . . thus, in our hypothetical case with four overtaking waves a minute, there would be between 5,000 and 6,000 pitching and oscillating movements of the hull in the course of a day, 35,000 to 40,000 a week, and more than 150,000 a month. Multiply these figures by the number of booms and gaffs participating in this motion and the problem of what becomes of all this energy must loom ever larger in our speculation . . . It is my contention that the incessant pumping action of the boom and gaffs of a big schooner sailing free in a following sea acts like just such a continually applied alternating stress further complicated, in all probability, by a reciprocating torque or twist component due to the unsymmetrical nature of the schooner rig.[13]

And, of course, as everyone who has sailed a dinghy knows, a gybe can be very dangerous. Here is an account of near disaster to the steel four-masted barquentine *Mozart* in the Southern Ocean from Captain Karl Kåhre, who was serving on board as a 'jungman' at the time. The master was his elder brother, Paul Kåhre,

> One thing even a first voyager in a barquentine very soon found out was how dangerous 'gybeing' was in the really big gaff riggers. We had a very bad reminder of that in heavy weather south of Good Hope. We were running before the wind with shortened sails down to upper and lower topsails on the foremast and of the gaffsails only the mizzen standing, the stormsail of the gaffsails. In the strong wind and heavy seas we were doing about 12 knots when the helmsman was not attentive enough of the course and the mizzen sail came gybeing with a terrible bang from starboard over to port. The boom broke the heavy vangtackle, the gaff broke in the middle when it came crushing into the port shrouds and the sail was torn from top to bottom. The helmsman and the mate on watch tried to prevent the gybeing with the result that the whole mess, the broken gaff, the boom and the torn sail all came thundering back to starboard side and the vessel went alongside the mountainous seas with her port side. Well, captain came on deck and all hands were called and we managed to brace wind into the squaresails and the vessel back on her course. Lucky enough we were lightly loaded with a cargo of timber from Sweden so we got very little water on deck. But what would have happened if the vessel should have been down on her marks with the seas sweeping over her and the crew when we tried to secure the damage. Maybe in night time in the dark? . . .
>
> And I am sure that if *Mozart* had been a wooden built vessel when the

above related episode happened I think we should have been very near disaster.[14]

All these weaknesses of the big schooner apply, of course, to her use under transoceanic sailing conditions, as opposed to the long range North American coastal trade for which she was developed where sea conditions tended to be more moderate. Even despite these weaknesses many transoceanic passages were successfully completed by big schooners between 1870 and 1939. In the business for which they were developed, the coastal trade of the United States and Canada with regular passages as long as that, say, between Bristol and the Canary Isles, and later in the Baltic trade, the big schooner was highly successful, while the two-master and the three-master, which did not have the same inherent weaknesses, consequent upon size, operated profitably and safely all over the world and in the North Atlantic trades throughout the year.

On the other hand the advantages of the schooner over the square rigged vessel, at least as far as the special trading conditions on the East Coast of North America are concerned, were summarised in an article in the American newspaper, *The Bath Independent* of Bath, Maine, in 1883,

The schooner is a very economical vessel; she costs less to build, because there are no yards to make and rig. The masts cost less. A smaller crew can handle her with equal safety. Did you ever watch a ship go about from one tack to another? What with rising tacks and sheets and bracing the yards and getting everything snug again, it is a job that is performed when the watch is called so that all hands can have a chance at the sport. Besides that, the ship while in stays often loses her headway and drifts astern a part of the time.

But when a schooner is beating to windward, the helm is put down by the man at the wheel. She comes up with her canvas shaking fore and aft. A man shifts the topsail tacks and the booms swing over. The mate looks on with his hands in his pockets. Two men only are on deck. She never loses headway for an instant, but gains several lengths every time she tacks. Once around she will run from one to two points nearer the wind and the ship. For the coastwise and the gulf trades schooners are unequalled. The most profitable size for the coast trade is one that will carry 800 or 900 tons of coal. For the West India trade larger ones are built, with great success. The whole question of rigging a ship is to get the necessary spread of canvas in the most convenient shape.

The readiness of the shipowners and masters of North America who developed the big schooner to accept innovation did not extend to adopting Forbes' staysail rig, which we now recognise as the best available at the period. Indeed, something very like it comprises the rig of the ultra-sophisticated four- and five-masted motor schooners and the four-masted barquentines which operate commercially in the 1990s in the cruise business in the Caribbean and the Mediterranean, the sails of which are entirely computer controlled. Nevertheless, they performed a remarkably creative adaptation in an environment which was intensely conservative and based upon materials such as wood and hemp and upon the basic technology of carpenter and blacksmith. For to understand the operation of the big schooner it is necessary to forget all the practices of traditional sailing ship seamanship, and the handling of square rigged vessels or the smaller schooners. The big schooner's success depended on ship handling and management of a kind in many ways entirely different from anything that had ever gone before.

In *The Illustrated American* of 1891 an article appeared which put the matter of the use of the donkey-engine very well:

Coincident with the development of size and rig has been the introduction of still more remarkable changes in the equipment of schooners, 'big ships require big crews', might have been an axiom twenty years ago, but it is not now, at least it is not applicable to these big schooners. Ten or possibly twelve men is the biggest crew required by any of them. The work of double or treble that number of men is done by machinery. A schooner is badly equipped indeed, now, that does not carry an engine to weigh the anchor, hoist the sails, and trim the sheets. As a shipowner tersely expressed it, 'The engine does everything but reef the sails, that is what the men are carried for'.

Later, when reasonably reliable oil engines were developed early in the present century, they were substituted for steam donkeys, a further economy since they could be operated without the licensed engineer required for the steam-donkey engine.

The sail area of a four-masted schooner was not almost infinitely flexible like that of a British-style three-master with her square topsails and easily reefed small fore and aft sails, or that of a barque with a whole series of different combinations of sails, small and large, open to the master. If the weather looked threatening, but uncertain, the master of a British schooner could carry his sails, knowing that if it came on to blow, he could take in his squaresails, take in the gaff topsails and reef his fore and afters relatively quickly. The master of a barque knew that he could relatively rapidly shorten down from his full complement of some twenty-four sails, and that at a pinch sail could be taken in in almost any normal weather conditions, should errors of judgement make it necessary for this to be done.

But the master of a four-masted schooner was faced with an entirely different situation. He could take in his gaff topsails and some of his headsails, but after that the next stage was reefing or taking in his four huge gaff and boom sails. This was a big job, carried out largely mechanically with the steam hoister, a process admitting of little flexibility. It could be done quickly but it could not be done in really bad conditions. If the sails were to be reefed the same process applied, because to handle such huge sails with a crew a large part of which was often relatively unskilled it was necessary to lower them altogether first and then bundle up the lower part of the sail in a reef while it was on deck and then reset the sail with the donkey-engine. The whole process of taking in the huge gaff sails was made much easier by the presence of a series of 'lazy jacks', heavy lines stretching from the mast head to the boom, inside which the sail neatly fell (in theory and usually in good weather) when the gaff was lowered. Nevertheless, if the big fore and afters were not got in in time they never could be got in at all and the canvas could be damaged perhaps beyond repair, which was an extremely expensive matter. So the master of a four-masted schooner had to be exceedingly weather-wise and had to look an even longer way ahead in making his decisions about what sail he should carry than most shipmasters.

The regular work aloft with the gaff topsails in these vessels was exacting and difficult. In the four-masters the gaff topsails were jib-headed, the long luff held to the topmast with mast hoops. The lower part of the luff, where it stretched down below the mainmast cap was, however, not secured to a jackstay (as it was in the very much smaller British vessels when the topsail was stowed aloft and not set from the deck) and so, set on the lee side, it tended to blow away from the masthead, which considerably reduced its efficiency. In order to make it stand to its work the tack of the topsail had to be shifted to the weather side of the gaff between the peak halyards and the gaff itself. The shape and the setting of these sails can clearly be seen in several of the photographs in this book, especially that of the *Gov. Ames.*

As has already been said, the mastheads were joined together by the triatic or jump stay which was an essential part of the whole rigging system on the big schooners. The gaff swung below this stay; the luffs of the topsails were secured to the topmasts with hoops above it, so that the lower part of the sail had to be lifted over the stay each time the vessel went round through the wind. In effect, the topsail had to be taken in and reset every time the ship went round. This meant that a hand aloft had to shift the heavy chain sheets, which (in the words of Captain Karlsson, who was speaking in English, and not his native Swedish), in the *Edward H. Cole* were 'the same size as the anchor chain of a small schooner'. The seaman had to haul the tack over the triatic stay and toss the coil of the tack line down to deck with a cry of 'sheet home' each time she went round. This work aloft on the bare fore and aft rigged masts, with little hand hold, required considerable physical strength, confidence and dexterity. It was one of the most difficult of all regular jobs aloft in any big sailing ship, though the exercise of taking in the gaff topsail in a small British or Scandinavian ketch, jumping about in a seaway, was even worse.

The big schooners required special handling. With their huge flat-floored hulls and long straight sides they took some time to get up speed, but, despite their weight, they stopped quickly when the wind was spilled from their sails. Because their simple and economical rigging did not present much windage they could, and frequently did, anchor, even on a lee shore, to ride out bad weather. Because of the steam hoister again, the anchors could be and were massive and with very heavy cables which made the technique relatively safe, particularly in the shallow waters of parts of the United States East Coast. It is possible that the loss of the great steel seven-masted *Thomas W. Lawson*, the largest merchant sailing vessel ever built, when her cables parted in a gale off the Scilly Isles was due partly to the fact that her Master was doing what he had done many times before in perfect safety on the New England coast, but that he had not allowed for the power of a full southwesterly gale in an exposed position on the east side of the North Atlantic.

John T Rowland wrote,

When the clippers passed, the crews of the square-rigged cargo carriers were cut to the minimum possible. To reduce these further without

decreasing the vessels' size, and at the same time turn out a ship which could make coasting voyages against contrary winds; to produce a sturdy flat-floored hull that would take no damage by beaching on the Fundy flats and yet could work to windward in a Hatteras gale, one which would be deep enough to ride out a blow at sea, yet able to ascend the shallow southern rivers, and finally to produce a sailing vessel on a large scale which, in spite of the conditions mentioned, could make a long deep water voyage in fair time when occasion demanded — there was a proposition to turn a designer's hair grey.

I may be getting ahead of myself, but right here I must tell you how well it has been answered by citing the case of a particular ship that I know. She is a four-masted schooner of 1400 tons dead-weight capacity (about 200 feet long o.a.) and she carries a complement of only nine people, all told. She has made a voyage from Axim, on the West Coast of Africa, to Boston in 60 days with a full cargo of mahogany logs; from Blue Hill, Maine, to Trinidad in about three weeks with three million barrel staves in her hold and on deck; from Trinidad to Mobile in 15 days with asphalt; and from Brunswick, Georgia, to New York in 11 days in midwinter with 612 ninety-foot sticks of piling on board. I have known her to beat into a narrow harbour in the West Indies and berth herself where there was no tug to help; I have seen her perched high and dry beside a Fundy dock with 1250 tons of rock in her hold, and I have known her to do her 10 knots, loaded, for three days running before an easterly gale, although that is her worst point of sailing . . .

For one who has been fond of navigating great waters in small yachts the big fore-and-after holds a paradoxical charm, because she is the nearest thing to a single-hander that exists above 30 feet in length. Far fetched this may sound, yet it is, in my experience, literally true.[15]

The quotation applies to the handy four-masters of 750 tons or so which represented the big schooner at its best. The medium size four-master carrying a thousand tons or so of cargo and built to a high specification under the conditions which were obtained on the coast of Maine in the early years of this century was among the most handsome, and certainly among the most efficient, wooden merchant sailing vessels ever to be constructed.

There is a lovely description of one of these four-masters by Henry Hughes of Porthmadog in North Wales, a man soaked in contemporary British square rigged sailing vessel technology, in his autobiographical book *Through Mighty Seas.*[16]

Following in the *Cleopatra*'s wake came an American coffee clipper, a 2,000 ton 4-masted fore and aft rigged sailing vessel, running between Rio and the northern States of America, carrying the world's most delicious coffee to the American people. They were lovely ships, and quite different from our ideas of clippers — 4 tall masts scraped and sun bleached, looking much like ivory. On these were set but 12 sails made of perfect material known as American cotton canvas and fitting faultlessly. Their spars and sails were the envy of the world. Black hulls, white deck fittings, and high bows, gave them a business like appearance; and they could sail.

Henry Hughes is in fact exaggerating the size of the four-master he saw. She was probably the *Doris*, one of four similar vessels, actually barquentine rigged, owned by Morton, Stewart & Co, all built at Belfast

Maine, for the South American coffee trade to Baltimore and noted, according to Captain W J Lewis Parker, as 'extremely handsome vessels – near to perfection in appearance'.[17]

This whole pattern of change and development was due to the intelligent use of the steam hoisting engine, without which there would have been no big schooners. Faced with the opportunities provided by steam, the shipping people, especially of the State of Maine, responded with enterprise and imagination.

The American maritime historian W H Bunting adopted a slightly romantic approach when he wrote:

> A society which created a vehicle as marvellous as the [Maine built three-masted schooner] *Lavinia Campbell* to carry its coal is also worthy of our consideration . . . The large Eastern coasting schooner was in many ways symbolic of the period between the Civil War and World War One, when American society was on the one hand irreversibly committed to a future of vast changes, while on the other still tied to traditions of ages past.[18]

That is one way to look at the phenomenon of the big schooner on the East Coast of North America. Another view, the economic historian's view if you like, is that after the Civil War, in a society intent on the frenetic exploitation of its own vast land resources, the big schooner represented in both economic and literal terms a very marginal operation. It was exploitation, quite often by out-of-state interests, of the fag end of New England's wooden shipbuilding and ship managing skills and resources, with the aid of the steam hoisting engine, to make relatively low profits with minimum capital investment out of the transient situation created by a southern coal mining industry, which had not yet got its land transport organised to the degree necessary to enable quick enough loading to make the employment of steel steam-driven tonnage profitable in coastwise transportation to the northern consumption points.

The multi-masted schooners built in eastern North America are frequently spoken of as the first of their kind. But it must be remembered that, before the successful application of the marine compound engine to crew steamers in the mid 1860s, fully powered merchant steam vessels were limited to relatively short voyage operations and they needed what is now called a 'sail assist' rig. Indeed, because of the difficulty of handling them in big seas and strong winds, sails were essential for the successful operation of paddle steamers on ocean voyages.[19] The designers and builders of these vessels showed enterprise, powers of innovation and a refreshing freedom from the bonds of traditionalism in the development of these sail assist rigs. There were three-masted, schooner rigged steamers at sea in the 1820s. In the 1830s the pioneering transatlantic liner the *Great Western* of Bristol had a sophisticated four-masted, schooner rig and may well have been the world's first four-masted, fore and aft rigged vessel. Certainly her successor, *The Great Britain* was the first vessel in history to be registered as a six-masted schooner and when the next six-master of comparable size was built, the *Wyoming* at Bath, Maine, in 1909, her rigging — for good economic reasons, perfectly comprehensible in the circumstances — was primitive in comparison with the sophistication of *The Great Britain*'s rigging and sail plan, which was the most advanced

ever put into a vessel at the time she was launched and for many years afterwards. But it is extremely unlikely that there was any cross-fertilisation between the sail-assist schooner rigs developed in Britain in the mid nineteenth century and the four-, five- and six-masted schooners developed in North America four decades later.

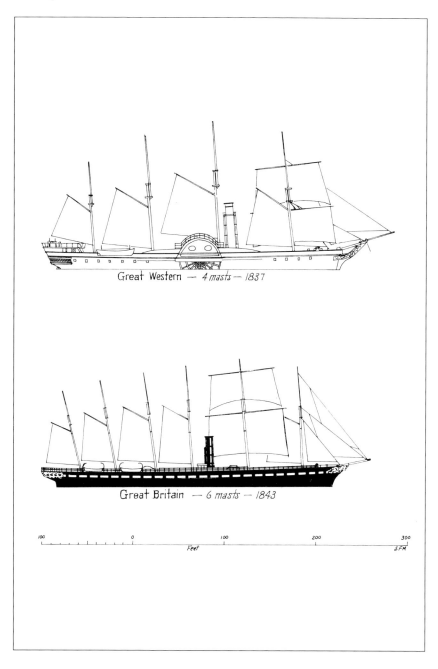

British sail-assist, multi-mast schooner rigs for early steamships. The Great Britain was the first vessel in history to be registered as a six-masted schooner, 66 years before the American-built Wyoming *(scale 1 inch = 100 feet)*

15

The background to the operation of the *Bertha L. Downs* and her sisters

It has to be said that in history, societies have not usually turned to the sea if there is an acceptable alternative means of life on land. In mid nineteenth-century New England limited fertile land in the coastal regions and limited industrialisation led to the development of a thriving merchant shipping industry, greatly stimulated by the Californian and Australian gold discoveries, by the opening up of the West Coast of the Continent, and by developments in world trade centred on industrial and financial expansion in Britain. This American merchant shipping industry was typically represented by the ubiquitous wooden brig, barque, or full rigged ship, built and owned in some small place between the Kennebec and the Passamaquoddy rivers in the State of Maine and to be met with anywhere the world's carrying trade took her. At the other extreme it was represented by the American clipper ships which made a serious, but short-lived, challenge to British shipping supremacy in the 1850s. As Geoffrey Safford put it:

> . . . American ships were managed and manned by capable personnel. In the people's conviction, embellished by the testimonials of the nations' literati, the magnificent clipper ships of the 1840s and 50s symbolised the triumphant genius of American shipping and ship-building, and perhaps as well the emotional psyche of the nation itself — frenetic energy and industry, brute strength, great size, expansion, and speed. Had any American, standing in the mid 1850s on a Boston harbour wharf, or on New York's Battery, dared to suggest that American shipping would soon wane dramatically, most likely he would have met with hostile disavowals, or, at best, statements of incredulity.[20]

As Safford pointed out there is evidence that the decline of the American merchant shipping industry had already begun well before the War Between the States but from the beginning of that war in 1860 it degenerated rapidly. To quote Safford again:

> Whereas in 1860 two-thirds of all export and import tonnage was carried in American bottoms, this had fallen by 1866 to 30% and nine years later to 27%. The decline continued at a precipitous rate; in 1881 it was 16% and in 1910 but 8.7%. On the eve of World War One of all vessels engaged in the world ocean carrying trade, only 2% were of American registry.

What had happened was that the War Between the States wreaked havoc on American shipping. A system of protective tariffs was instituted. The War left a triumphant industrialising north and a shattered rural south. Only four years later the transcontinental railroad was completed. The Continent could at last be opened up. Rapid industrialisation and phenomenal immigration leading to explosive population growth meant an almost infinitely big home market and relatively little export trade for American ships to carry. During the War nearly half the deepwater fleet had been destroyed, sold, or transferred to foreign flags. This was the crucial period when the high-pressure compound engine in the iron steamship was making, at last, the beginning of the end of the wooden sailing ships of the British merchant shipping industry. The high

local cost of iron prohibited the building of compound engined steamers in the United States and there were more lucrative and less hazardous investment opportunities to hand in the post Civil War world. Money and men turned from the sea to industry, railroads, real estate, and the West. The West indeed provided trades in which the big wooden square rigged sailing vessel prospered for a couple more decades, but British compound engine steamers and steel sailing vessels were highly competitive and the American 'down easters', as the great full rigged ships of the 1870s and 1880s were called, ceased to be built in significant numbers after the middle of the 1880s.

However, the industrial expansion, which was one of the factors in the demise of America's deep-sea merchant marine, proved to be a boon to the development of the long-range coastal trade of the Atlantic ports. Under legislation dating back to 1817 foreign flag vessels were not allowed to trade between American ports and no foreign-built vessel, even though American owned and registered, could carry cargoes in the coastal trades. Bearing in mind the low costs of operating sail-driven tonnage in bulk trades at this period it is not perhaps surprising that after the War Between the States the coastal trade prospered mightily and greater tonnage was 'enrolled' in the coasting trade than was 'registered' for foreign trade.[21] Thus sheltered from competition the coasting trade did not share the catastrophic decline of the deepwater trades. The building and operation of screw-propelled, bulk-carrying steamers did not develop rapidly in United States' waters and, for reasons already given, foreign built vessels could not be purchased for the coastal trades. Sailing vessels in the coastal trades were therefore not subject to the same competitive pressure of steamships as were the deepwater vessels. It was, in fact, not until 1894 that steam tonnage exceeded that of sail tonnage in United States' coastal shipping. Even in 1900 the tonnage of the American coastwise fleet was five times as large as that of the deepwater fleet, and sailing vessels represented nearly half of it.

After the War Between the States the sailing vessels almost universally employed in the coastal trade were wooden schooners and the principal part of the trade was in coal from Virginia to New England. This trade grew very rapidly in the three decades after 1865 until by 1900 nearly five million tons of coal, nearly all water-borne and much of it from Virginia, was imported into Boston alone.

This coal was used for many purposes. The town's gas industry consumed a vast quantity of coal and after gas was supplanted by electricity for lighting purposes, gas cookers and furnaces were introduced. At the same time the network of electric street car routes (trams in Britain) was being developed in New England to the point at which, it is said, it was possible to travel, with many changes between vehicles, all the way from New York city to Boston by street car. All this development as well as the development of industry meant a growing demand for coal backed up by the demands of the expanding railroad system.

The biggest factor in favour of the sailing vessel in the coal trade was the inadequacy of loading facilities. The trade expanded too rapidly for rail and dock facilities to keep pace. Schooners were frequently delayed for a week or more while coal came down from the pits. With their low overheads they could afford these delays: steamers could not. In 1909 when facilities for loading were greatly improved the days of the schooner were suddenly limited and new construction came virtually to a stop.

As the demand for coal expanded almost explosively the small schooners of the 1860s were quite unable to handle the ever-increasing demand. In 1870 the average three-masted schooner could carry about 350 tons but there were already big vessels with a cargo capacity running up to about 1200 tons.[22] Soon even these vessels were quite unable to carry profitably coal shipments of the size in current demand, for they could not show the net returns of bigger vessels utilising the economies of scale. After 1880 four-masters were built, a few of which by 1890 had a cargo capacity of 2500 tons. The first five-master on the Atlantic coast (there was an earlier five-master, the *David Dows*, built on the Great Lakes in 1883), the *Gov. Ames*, already referred to, was launched at Waldoboro, Maine, in 1888. She was originally intended as a four-master, but the decision was taken during her building to give her an additional mast, because, in the words of her first master and principal shareholder, Captain Cornelius A Davis,

> as a four-master her sails would have been very large, so we decided to put in the fifth mast which divided the length into five sails and made each sail easier to handle and the sails last longer.[23]

The *Gov. Ames* had a very successful career, after the setback of the early dismasting, carrying coal cargoes of up to 3000 tons until her loss off Cape Hatteras in 1909.

The development of the big schooner on the East Coast of the United States appears to have taken place by a simple process of growth in size. As illustrated by Captain Davis' remark quoted above, when a new vessel was planned with greater cargo capacity than her predecessors, another mast was added. Thus in 1900 the first two six-masters to be built in North America were launched, the larger of which, the *Eleanor A. Percy*, could load about 5500 tons of coal. These huge schooners, with each mast rigged in the tradition of the early three-masters, had their weaknesses, as has already been explained, but the likely advantages of R B Forbes' proposed staysail rig were not seen as outweighing the trouble and cost of the research and experiment which would have to have proceeded their development. The conservative seaboard communities of Maine, where the majority of the big schooners were launched, were not prepared to hazard risk capital in the development of new types of rigging.

There were many other trades besides the coal trade. The re-discovery of the fact that ice could be carried great distances with good profit and without ruinous losses of the cargo led to a thriving trade between the Kennebec river and Pennobscot Bay ports and the towns of the coasts to the south. Charles S Morgan summed up the complexity of the schooners' trades very well in the 37th Annual Newcomen Lecture which was delivered at the United States Coast Guard Academy, New London, Connecticut, in November, 1978.

> Both sides of the Kennebec above Bath were lined with enormous ice houses where the winter ice harvest was stored against summertime

demand. The shipment of ice, almost entirely in schooners, grew from 30,000 tons in 1860 to 3,000,000 tons in 1880. Twenty years later the export ice trade had all but vanished.

There was an interesting relationship between the coal and ice trades. The coal ports from New York to Newport News provided a good market for ice and many a schooner had profitable round voyages carrying ice one way and coal the other.

Urban expansion with its construction of tenements and suburban homes just prior to and following the turn of the century produced a vigorous trade for schooners in the carriage of lumber and laths. Piling was in demand for piers, wharves, and utility poles while railroad ties were moved in vast quantities from southern ports to northern and eastern railroad centres. The shipyards in Maine and elsewhere where schooners were built had to import the materials as local stands of oak, pine, and hackmatack had long since been exhausted. Thus schooners loaded oak ship timber and pine planking in the south and delivered it to New England shipyards where it was converted into more vessels. Hackmatack knees were imported from the Maritime Provinces and mast timber brought round or overland from the Pacific Northwest. To facilitate handling long timber and lumber cargoes, schooners were equipped with rectangular bowports in to the 'tween decks and lower hold spaces to supplement the large deck hatches which were characteristic.

Hard pine was loaded at a great many ports, large and small, between Wilmington, N.C., and Mississippi gulf ports; its destination: anywhere North of Cape Hatteras. Consumption was enormous not only for dwelling and ship construction but also in new mills, bridges and railroad trestles. Phosphate rock, important as an ingredient of agricultural fertiliser, began to be shipped North from Charleston in the 1870s. Huge deposits of it were discovered in central Florida in the '90s and this opened up a new opportunity for schooners, loading at Port Tampa and Punta Gorda. The rock was carried to fertiliser plants in Baltimore, New York, to points on the Delaware, to Norfolk, Virginia and to North Weymouth, Massachusetts. The trade had its attractions such as freights at $2.50 per ton when coal was bringing 65–75 cents. But it also had its drawbacks such as its great weight, requiring careful stowage, and its propensity to absorb water, thus thwarting the pumps. This business also exposed vessels to the hazards of hurricanes in the passage around Florida. Nevertheless many four-masted schooners enjoyed a nice two-way trade carrying coal from Baltimore to Galveston for the Texas railroads and ships' bunkers and returning with phosphate rock from Port Tampa or railroad ties from Mobile, Fernandina or Jacksonville. . . .

The production of granite was a leading Maine industry for many years and a fleet of small two- and three-masted schooners moved it to Boston, New York, Philadelphia and Washington where there was an increasing need for it in public buildings, monuments, roads and kerbings.

It should be noted that schooners made many voyages to South America and the West Indies with lumber, coal, and general cargo returning with hides and bones, linseed, salt from Turks Island, or logwood from Haiti. Though not strictly coastal passages such off-shore trips were very common. Indeed it was the goat manure trade from Venezuela to Jacksonville and Baltimore fertiliser plants that kept the few surviving schooners alive down to the time of World War Two.[24]

With such a complex pattern of trades available, besides the steady standby of the coal trade, it is perhaps not surprising that there were at least 458 four-masted schooners launched on the Eastern and Gulf Coasts of the United States.[25] In addition some 36 four-masters came round Cape Horn from the West Coast and operated on the Atlantic and Gulf Coasts, so there were at least 494 four-masted schooners operating on the East Coast of the United States. There were in addition 37 four-masters built in Canada and one built in the Bahamas, so this makes a grand total of 531 four-masters. Between 1879 and 1921 over 1500 three-masters were built, 45 five-masters and 10 six-masters. The great majority of the bigger vessels were built in the State of Maine.

The East Coast schooners were mostly run individually as single corporate enterprises, the vessel property divided into sixty-four shares spread over perhaps forty owners or more with a managing owner who was the inspiration of the enterprise of 'getting up a vessel', as the local saying in Maine had it. There were exceptions, of which the most conspicuous was William Palmer, a former schoolmaster who moved from Taunton, Massachusetts, to Boston and set up as the managing owner of what was to become the largest American schooner fleet. He was an extrovert personality and his schooners were picked out from the generality of vessels by white paint, immaculately maintained rigging, sails and spars, and by the word 'Palmer' which occurred as part of the name of each vessel. As manager, William Palmer usually held only one or two 64ths in each schooner. In addition to the dividends on these shares Palmer received 2 per cent of the gross earnings, a monthly wage in respect of each vessel, brokerage on charters and a fee for overseeing the building of each vessel. His fellow shareholders included men in the shipping industry who stood to profit from providing services to the vessel, the master, who was required to own three shares, at least, all the time he was in command, members of the extended Palmer family and close friends. These shareholders did quite well. In 1903 the average yield to shareholders was 21 per cent. This was a good year and the fleet average over the years was more like 12 per cent. The most profitable vessel was the five-masted *Rebecca Palmer* which between her launch in 1901 and 1909 paid 17 per cent per annum.[26]

The masters of the schooners were usually native-born Americans who, after perhaps a high-school education, started their careers before the mast in small vessels. They progressed to second mate and to first mate, moving to larger schooners and when they had enough experience and had saved sufficient capital to buy a master's interest, providing they had good connections and friends they were able to take command. Until 1898 no master's licence was required to take charge of a sailing vessel in the coastal trade but in that year a federal law required masters of sailing vessels of 700 or more tons to be licensed. It is not surprising perhaps that this legislation was followed by the building of many 699-ton schooners with, as Charles Morgan wrote:

> enough obvious difference between them to suggest that there was a lot of slippage in the hand holding the measuring tape when the vessel was measured for documentation.[27]

Charles Morgan goes on,

> Masters of schooners were generally compensated in one of two ways. Prior to the turn of the century a system known as 'shares' or 'square halves' was most common. Under this plan the port charges were paid from the gross freight. The remainder was then divided equally between the Master and the vessel. Capital expenditure such as sails and repairs came out of the vessel's share and whatever was left accrued to the owners as dividends. The Captain paid the crew's wages and subsistence and kept what was left. When vessels became very large and costly to build Masters were generally engaged at wages of $40–$50 per month plus 5% of the gross earnings, a system known as 'wages and primage'. . . .
>
> The annual income of the Master of a large five-masted coal schooner during the first decade of the twentieth century can be approximated by working from a few assumptions. If we assume that the schooner could make ten trips a year, each one carrying 5,000 tons of coal at an average freight of 80 cents per ton, the primage at 5 would amount to $2,000. Add wages of $600 and perhaps $250 in dividends on his share and his total income reaches $2,850. In terms of purchasing power this compares to about $30,000 today [that was in 1978 and would be a good deal more in the 1990s].

In the nineteenth century the majority of the crews of schooners were native-born Americans, but as the years went by many other opportunities for employment opened up in the United States. The crews changed to mixed foreign-born, often Scandinavian and Nova Scotian. In due course West Indians and Cape Verdians joined the schooners. Karl Victor Karlsson of Grunsunda, Wårdö, in the Åland Islands of Finland, who was to become master of the *Bertha L. Downs* as the *Atlas* when she was sailing under the Finnish flag, told me of his early experience of the handling of the big American schooners when, in 1917, he was an able seaman on board the *Edward H. Cole*, a very large four-master built at Rockland, Maine, in 1904. The crew were all Scandinavians, plus two Finns, and there was only one native-born United States citizen on board. Some of the Scandinavians had been sailing in big American schooners for thirty years. The *Cole* was a large vessel, loading about 3000 tons of cargo. Big gaff and boom sails were nothing new to Karlsson, who had had two seasons in the barquentine *Nils* working in the Baltic timber trade, but everything on board the *Cole* was on a relatively vast scale. Although she was nearly a new vessel she was utterly dependent on her steam pumps, which were kept going all the time to keep her afloat. The donkeyman was an old Swede.[28]

The particular interest of these big schooners rests partly in the fact that they represent almost the only point of contact between the big wooden merchant sailing vessel and the modern world of power, technology and something like civilised living and working conditions for the crew. Economic coincidences led to their development as the very end product of the centuries when the wooden sailing vessel represented the only means of carriage at sea. They survived into the fifth decade of the twentieth century. The last four-master working at sea, the *Herbert L. Rawding*, by then heavily motorised, was lost at sea in June 1947. In July 1948 the

Canadian-built three-master *Frederick P. Elkin* was the last schooner ever to load coal at the Newport News wharves.[29] She sailed for Barbados and survived in the inter-island trade into the 1950s.[30]

Nothing quite like these big schooners developed in Europe, although a few vessels were built which were influenced by the big American schooners, though more of the type developed on the Pacific Coast rather than in the New England States. It is not surprising, therefore, that when they visited European ports the big American schooners aroused very great interest. In fact, over the years considerable numbers of East Coast-built United States and Canadian schooners made transatlantic voyages with lumber, oil in barrels or cases, tobacco or guano or salt fish. They returned with Welsh coal, or with salt for the New England fisheries or fruit for New York or Boston. In the year 1876 alone no fewer than 233 transatlantic voyages were made by American three-masted schooners and there was scarcely a European port from the Baltic to the Mediterranean where they were not to be seen. These transatlantic passages continued steadily through the generations and were still being made by Canadian schooners in some numbers in the 1920s and 1930s. Among the last to be made by American vessels were those of the four-masted *Helen Barnet Gring* and the five-masted *Edna Hoyt* just before the Second World War.

The first five-master to cross the Atlantic was the *Rebecca Palmer*, already mentioned, on her maiden voyage. As soon as she had been fitted out she sailed from Rockland, Maine, for New York City where she loaded 14,500 barrels of naptha which she had been chartered to carry to Havre and Rouen. Because of the dangerous nature of her cargo the steam hoister's furnace was not fired and it must have taken a very long time — probably at least a day of very hard work for her total crew of fifteen including the master and the mates — to set the five lowers by hand hauling. It was perhaps fortunate that only one sail had to be taken in on the twenty-five day passage to Havre.

Having sailed from New York on 14 May she arrived at Havre on 7 June 1901. In Rouen, far up the river Seine, she was fêted as not only the first five-master but also the largest vessel ever to have discharged at the port. She was the subject of a good deal of press attention. Her master, Captain Sumner, was presented by the local Chamber of Commerce with a medal to commemorate the occasion. Having discharged the residue of her cargo the *Rebecca Palmer* sailed for Plymouth in England on 28 June and arrived on 30 June. Here she loaded 1200 tons of china clay. When she sailed a local newspaper waxed lyrical. Describing the departure from Plymouth of part of the British fleet the correspondent wrote,

> There was a little time of waiting, and it was nearly six o'clock before the masts and funnel of the first big ship appeared around Devil's Point. Then came on, one after another, gliding slowly and gracefully round the curve that clears Drake's Island, and so past the Breakwater Lighthouse and on to Torbay or Portland. 'No nation can touch us in that', said a proud spectator, and such like remarks might have been heard from many a little knot of those who watched the vessels pass by. Certainly they made a group, from a spectacular point of view, at least, of which the greatest Sea Power in the world had no reason to be ashamed.

And yet perhaps to a painter's eye — say Turner's, if he were yet alive — there would have seemed more beauty and stateliness in the large ship which immediately preceded the warships out of the harbour. This was the fine American five-masted sailing ship *Rebecca Palmer*. She was in tow of two tugs that seemed but toys beside her, and with her shining white hull and tall, straight row of masts she looked the very picture of symmetry. She bore proudly aloft the Stars and Stripes, and this combination of the American flag with the British flags on the warships, in the same coup d'oeil in a harbour associated so closely with the history of both nations, was as striking as it was picturesque.[31]

The *Rebecca Palmer* was towed round to Fowey, an ancient seaport in the adjacent county of Cornwall and about thirty miles from Plymouth by sea. Here she attracted a good deal of attention. The *Western Morning News* again carried an enthusiastic item:

> The fine new five-masted ship *Rebecca Palmer*, of Boston, which was towed round from Plymouth to Fowey on Tuesday evening, is now in harbour at the latter place to take in some 1,500 tons or more of china clay, in addition to the 1,200 tons which she loaded at Plymouth. The ship has been visited by a number of people every day at Fowey. She is the largest vessel ever seen in the harbour, and the fourth largest of her class in the world. Under the courteous guidance of Captain Sumner, we had an opportunity on Thursday of looking over the ship. She measures nearly 300 feet in length, and when sailing light the point of her jib stands 80 feet out of the water. The principal of her three decks runs right through almost from stem to stern. Built throughout of wood, her frame is of oak, and all the beams and 'knees' are of the most solid kind. The captain's cabin and the two or three adjoining state-rooms are beautifully floored in oak, and panelled in a variety of ornamental woods, including mahogany, bird's eye maple and pitchpine. All the carpets and furnishings are of the best and newest, and the bathroom, fitted with the latest devices of American ingenuity, is quite a feature.
>
> The most noteworthy thing about the ship, however, is the employment of steam power for hoisting the sails, handling the cargo and all such auxiliary purposes, the effect of which typically American economy is that the ship carries only a crew of thirteen all told — the captain and engineer included. Of course, the fore-and-aft rig of the ship in itself simplifies matters, but those accustomed to the old order of things on board ship would not be surprised at a vessel of the kind requiring thirty or thirty-five hands to man her. Captain Sumner shews with pardonable pride a fine gold medal presented to him by the Chamber of Commerce at Rouen (his first voyage across from New York was to Havre and Rouen) as a souvenir of the ship's visit to that port. Our Plymouth Chamber, which very properly welcomes the arrival of any noteworthy new steam liner, might have done well to take a little notice of the *Rebecca Palmer*, but the opportunity slipped by, probably just because no one happened to think of it.

The reference to the small number of hands bears on the reported expectations of local shops of a roaring trade in souvenirs and so forth with the crew of forty or so who would have been needed to handle a well manned five-masted barque of the period. They were disappointed also to find the vessel fully provisioned and even with an adequate supply of water for the return voyage. The correspondent of the *Lostwithiel & Fowey Guardian* recorded some of his impressions:

> There are no yards on either of the masts, consequently there is little work to be done aloft. After getting all the information from the Captain I thanked him, and leaving him in the cabin, where a number of visitors were flowing, I again joined the first mate on deck, and then glancing upward at her tall gaunt looking masts, I thought, is it possible that such a huge, strongly-built vessel as this seemed to be, could become crippled and dismantled, and driven to perdition by the treacherous winds and waves, which so suddenly spring up in mid-ocean. The mate took me for'ard, where I saw the kitchen and mess-room adjoining. The kitchen is fitted out with all necessary utensils, the water from the tanks below being raised by a powerful pump. I drank of the water, which was taken from Boston in March last, and I found it cool and mellow, and quite equal in taste to our water here. Going further for'ard, we went down into another room and pointing to a heap of machinery, the mate said, 'This is the man that does the work'. He then explained the various axles and pumps which did the raising of sails and anchors, and water for the scrubbing of decks. The first mate who, with the skipper, are the only two Americans on board, [the rest of the crew comprised Swedes, Germans and Belgians, many of them no doubt hopeful of acquiring American citizenship in due course] was extremely nice, and whilst in his company he spoke to the crew in such a manner that lead me to believe that he was far from being a bully, which some of these officers so often boast themselves of being. After spending something over an hour on board, I bade him 'good day' and left the ship, feeling delighted at having had such a splendid opportunity of seeing this ponderous structure, one of the latest novelties from the ship-building yards of our go-ahead cousins across the herring pond.[32]

While she took on a further 1500 tons of china clay the *Rebecca Palmer* received many visitors, including Sir Arthur Quiller Couch, then famous as an author, who presented Captain Sumner with a copy of his biography of the American Admiral Farragut. In the words of the *Boston Journal*'s report of the round voyage,

> Meanwhile excursion trains were being run on the railroads from the interior to Fowey bringing people to see the American schooner, and for days her decks were crowded with interested and curious people, who were amazed at the lace curtained windows of the cabin, the beautiful finish of the captain's apartments and the novelties of a Yankee vessel. It was a great day for the American merchant marine, in that little English harbor, and they learned many things about our ships which should have a tendency to teach them that Britannia does not rule the seas as she once did.
>
> But all things must have an end, and so the *Rebecca Palmer* on Aug. 1, spread her white wings and sailed from hospitable Fowey toward the land of the sun-set, and in thirty days was in New York Harbour, thence she came to Boston, her home port.[33]

The *Rebecca Palmer* had the longest life of any vessel of the Palmer fleet. As late as 1923 she was sold to Greek owners and broken up in the latter part of that year.[34] Her active life of twenty-two years compared very favourably with the twelve-year average life of the 45 five-masted schooners built on the East Coast of the United States between 1889 and the end of 1908.

The big American wooden schooners on the East Coast had a different history from the last British steel sailing ships. The industrial boom which followed the Spanish-American War of 1898, with other factors, led to great revival in the construction for the East Coast coal trade and other trades. In the coal trade which, despite their employment with so many other types of cargo, remained the backbone of the operation of these big schooners, the inadequacy of the facilities available at the coal-loading ports and the irregularity with which the coal supplies came down to the wharves from the pits still operated to the schooners' advantage. The trade had expanded too rapidly for railway and dock facilities to keep pace. In this trade, vessels were loaded in strict order of arrival at the ports and through pressure and through legal action the schooner owner succeeded in maintaining this practice well into the twentieth century. So the schooner continued to prosper and develop and took further step forward, in competition with trains of towed barges in the coasting trade.

However, in 1909 the Virginian railway was opened for the sole purpose of transporting coal from the new West Virginia coal fields to Norfolk for shipment. Its tidewater piers had the largest loading capacity in the world and brought to an end the delays in loading which had precluded the employment of steamers in the New England trades. The effect was decisive. In 1909 the launch of six four-masters and of the mighty *Wyoming*, marked the end of schooner-building until the resurrection during the First World War. During the First World War shipping boom in the eastern United States 133 four-masters were launched, ten five-masters, many big three-masters, and a dozen or more very big barquentines. In eastern Canada, 323 schooners were built, the great majority of them three-masters, but with a dozen or more four-masters and at least two barquentines. Freight rates were very high and paid in advance and some of these wartime-built vessels did extremely well. Those launched early enough changed hands at extremely high prices. They were sold and re-sold at many times their book value and often sent across to France with war supplies at very high rates. For instance the 800-ton four-master *Carrie A. Lane*, built way back in 1887 at Bath, Maine, was bought in 1902 by A F Green of Rockland, Maine for $18,000. She was sold in January 1917 for $38,000. She had paid dividends of a total of $44,352 which, with the profits on the sale of the vessel, represented an investment paid back in full and an average profit of 43 per cent per year. She was lost under her new ownership in March 1918 on the Ivory Coast of Africa. Charles Morgan quotes a nice case of the same kind. The four-master *Nancy Hanks* was built at Thomaston in 1917 for a contract price of $110,000. Before she was completed she was sold for $150,000. Her first voyage was to South Africa with general cargo for which her owners drew a pre-paid freight of $225,000. This story could be repeated many times.

But after the war, the world's shipyards met the world demand for tonnage, steam and motor, much more quickly than many shipowners and investors had thought remotely possible and many of those whose vessels were delivered after 1919 were very badly caught out. As some fortunes had been made, so other fortunes were lost as sail tonnage rapidly depreciated in value in the face of collapsing freight markets. The new world of big sailing vessels withered away almost as quickly as it had blossomed forth. Nevertheless, it was this wartime building which ensured that in a limited number of trades a number of the big schooners, bought at prices far below their construction cost, were able to make not only a living but a reasonable profit through the 1920s and 1930s. Their story came to an end only with the Second World War.

The building of the *Bertha L. Downs*

One State, Maine, stands out as the greatest builder of big schooners. There were no less than 74 builders in operation at various times in Maine, who, between them, built 327 four-masted schooners. Of these builders nineteen were located on the banks of the Kennebec River in the neighbourhood of Bath. Between them they launched 162 four-masters in addition to five- and six-masted schooners.

Of these builders the most productive was the New England Shipbuilding Company, called, after 1889, the New England Company, which, between 1884 and 1906 launched 305 vessels, 38 of them four-masted schooners.[35] In 1906 the New England Company ceased to build vessels and Edward W Hyde of Bath leased part of the yard to build two schooners, the *Bertha L. Downs* and the *Mary Manson Gruener*, for the Benedict Manson Marine Company of New Haven, Connecticut.

The *Bertha L. Downs*, like virtually all the big United States East Coast schooners, was built to dimensions ultimately derived from a laminated half model carved out by an established modeller. He was not the Master Builder but a man who made part of his living from modelling schooners, that is by creating in three dimensions the basis of their design. He was quite likely a gifted pattern maker from one of the local foundries — the two trades seem to have gone together in New England. The half model was on a scale of ¼in to 1ft and it represented one half of the *Bertha L. Downs*, sliced down amidships fore and aft from the deck to the keel. It was not carved from a solid block but was an artificially assembled baulk of timber made up from layers of fine white pine planking, each layer 1½ in thick. The layers were fastened together with wooden pins driven into holes drilled right through the whole block, so that it was so strong that it could be handled and carved with chisels as easily as a piece of solid timber.

This half model largely determined the shape of the finished vessel, so it was extremely important. It could be judged by those responsible for building the vessel: the Master Builder, the principal sponsor of the vessel, and the future master who was, as we have seen, almost certainly a shareholder of the vessel. They judged it visually and tactilely, that is by drawing the tips of their fingers over the surface of the model. This was the best way of detecting irregularities and kinks in the developed curves, not readily detectable visually, which would loom enormously large in the finished vessel. This half model determined the basic all-important characteristics of the new vessel — how she would sail, how fast she would be, how seaworthy, how much cargo she could carry. It is not too much to say that the half model determined the very viability of the

Bertha L. Downs as a working merchant ship. It is quite likely that the model itself was chiselled and sandpapered here and there until a shape was achieved which satisfied everybody.

Drawings were not usually used in the building of the big schooners. Today we think on paper, or increasingly through the computer, but in New England in 1908 when the *Bertha L. Downs* was beginning to take shape on the bank of the Kennebec River at Bath — the site is still visible today, overgrown with bushes and small timber — the men concerned with the building of these vessels thought of her in three dimensions from the very beginning and there was no question of the literally dozens, perhaps hundreds, of drawings which would accompany such a project now, much less the computerised cutting out machinery for the frame and timber shapes which almost certainly would go with the building of big wooden ships today — if any such vessels were being launched anywhere in the world.

The process of developing the half model into a full sized schooner was extremely complex and we have described it in detail elsewhere.[36]

Briefly to summarise, the wooden pins that held the layers of the laminated half model together were knocked out so that it fell apart into its separate layers. Each of these on its top surface represented in shape a 'waterline' of the vessel — a shape at a given depth if she was sliced horizontally. By measuring the width of each of the layers of the half model in turn, first amidships and then the same distance for each layer forward and aft of the midships, and plotting the measurements scaled up to full size on the wooden floor of one of the New England Company's sheds and, subsequently, on a wooden floor laid on each side of the keel of the vessel when this had been laid, the rough shape of the main frames of the vessel could be scribed out in scratches made in the soft wood of the floor. Each of the breadths of the layers of the half model in turn would be laid off, scaled up to full size from the centreline which represented the vertical centre of the vessel from mid keel to mid deck. In this way the shape of the frames of the vessel — that is, the ribs of her skeleton — would be determined. It will be obvious from the foregoing that the half model represented the dimensions of the frames, that is the skeleton of the vessel and not those of the fully planked-up schooner.

The *Bertha L. Downs* and her sisters the big American multi-masted schooners were the only large, wooden merchant sailing ships in history built in relatively highly capitalised, well-equipped and well-organised big yards equipped with a great deal of machinery. The first stage in building a vessel was for the yard to order the timber necessary for her construction. Prodigious quantities of wood were needed to build even a medium size four-masted schooner like the *Bertha L. Downs*. This lumber came from all over the eastern States and much further afield. Hackmatack was cut up in Aroostook County of Maine, in Nova Scotia, in Prince Edward Island and in far away Michigan and sent by sea or rail to the shipyard. The frames of the *Bertha L. Downs* were made up of oak for the lower timbers, the floors and first futtocks, with hackmatack for the upper futtocks. Hackmatack was strong, lighter than oak, and much more resistant to rot in the vulnerable topsides of the schooner. 'Moulds', that is timber patterns made in the mould loft from the full size drawings scribed out on the floor from the half model, were supplied to the timber contractors and taken by them into the woods so that individual pieces of timber for the finished ship could be roughed out there with axes from newly felled trees. In this way the amount of timber transported, and consequently transport costs, were kept to a minimum. Small schooners took these patterns down to the south to get timbers from derelict plantations in Virginia and eastern Delaware. Some schooners were engaged almost entirely in taking down lumber gangs from Maine to this work, bringing back the semi-completed frames, already roughly shaped in the woods. Hard pine came from Georgia and South Carolina. Here families from Maine had already established saw mills.

The next stage in construction was the laying of the keel and the erection of the sternpost and counter framing and the stem on the keel. The critical work of assembling and erecting the frames then began. Double sawn frames were used in building the *Bertha L. Downs*. Each frame comprised in fact a pair of frames, each assembled out of as many as sixteen to eighteen pieces of timber and carefully matched and then fastened together to create a cross-section of the hull form at the appropriate point. These pairs of frames, each constituent part of which depended on its pair for strength and continuity in construction, were secured together with wooden pins and kept separate by spacing blocks to permit air circulation and hinder rot.

As soon as a reasonable number of frames had been erected along a portion of the keel the keelson was fitted to clamp the keel, frames, and keelson together. The keelson was a main strength member in a big

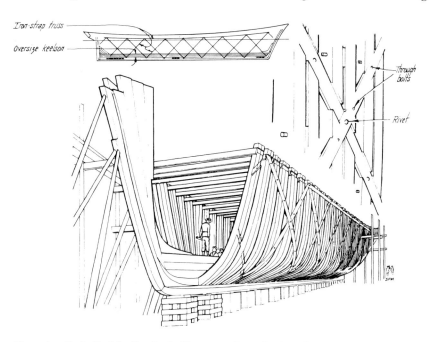

Strapping the hull of the Bertha L. Downs: *schematic view also showing the end of the keelson. The diagonal straps join a belt-strap along the sheer at the deck line. Their lower ends are bolted together and to the framework just under the turn of the bilge.*

schooner. In the case of the *Bertha L. Downs* the keelson was built up o 24in square Oregon pine baulks, bolted right through to the keel and bui up 6ft high.

When the skeleton of the keel, sternpost, stem, frames and keelson wa complete the deck beams could be fitted. In the case of the *Bertha L. Down* there was one set of these at main deck level. The bigger schooners – larger four-masters and the five- and six-masters — had two decks.

The complex process of planking could then begin. The planking of th *Bertha L. Downs* was all of pitch pine and no length in it was of less tha 40ft. This planking was massive by the standards of smaller woode ships, some of it 6in by 8in in size. Much of the planking was secured t the frames with wooden pins — 'treenails'. Some 20,000 treenails wer required for a big schooner and the yard had a separate treenail-makin, shop with power driven lathes which could do this work quite quickly There was also a large blacksmith's shop capable of handling the 200 o 300 tons of iron and steel which were needed for the building of a vesse like the *Bertha L. Downs*. Iron was needed for bolts, nails, chain plates an mast ironwork, amongst other things.

There was also a separate oakum shop. Here the caulkers could spi their raw materials in wet weather. The *Bertha L. Downs* had five or si miles of seaming between her planks to be caulked. On a basis of fou threads to each seam, each thread divided into loops, about 48 miles o oakum had to be spun and driven — work for twelve to fifteen me labouring six days a week for approximately three months. Near th oakum shop there was a pitch oven. Pitch wax was used for paying th deck. Frequently, the planking of the bottom was payed with Portlan cement, above the waterline with white lead putty. These practices wer very different from those used in European yards.

Once the planking was complete the 'ceiling' or interior planking wa fitted. This ceiling served as longitudinal reinforcement for the hull an was not only fastened right through the frames but often each of th adjoining strakes were fastened to each other with through bolts. Th ceiling was usually even more massive than the outside planking.

Once the hull was complete the masts were stepped and rigged. Th lower masts were about 120ft long and over 2ft 6in in diameter wher they were stepped on the keel. The liftings of these huge masts int position was done with the use of shearlegs and it was an heroic busines involving the greatest possible skill. The rigging, like most of the work o these big schooners, was done by sub-contractors; the riggers when the moved in to do a job gave demonstrations of skill and daring which muc impressed those who saw them at work. They worked 150ft above th deck without any kind of safety equipment and had a habit of gettin from mast to mast by going hand over hand along the horizontal wir stay which linked the heads of the huge lower masts. Frank A Palmer wa the leading rigging contractor in Bath at the time of the building of th *Bertha L. Downs*. Because the work, like the rigging, was sub-contracte most of the work force present in the yard at any one time answered no to the yard management but to the sub-contractors. The sub-contractor used the yard facilities, but built up, paid and controlled their own wor forces. The greater part of the labour force of the yard at the building o the *Bertha L. Downs* therefore did not regard themselves as yard workers but as skilled craftsmen who might work anywhere where employment was available. Men were able to make a good living simply out of shaping the frames and could command wages of as much as four dollars a day. These workers followed the demand for labour from shipyard to shipyard.

A specialist trade was that of 'inboard joiner'. These men were responsible not only for the elegant joinery in the after quarters, where the captain, mates and steward lived, and for the fitting out of the deck house forecastle, but also for the actual construction of all wooden deck structures, including deck houses, hatches, railings and supporting stanchions. On the *Bertha L. Downs* the crew lived in a deckhouse forecastle with a galley in the same structure, so that the food could be passed through a hatch and eaten hot. This galley was exceptionally large and has been described by Captain Karlsson, one day to command the vessel, as 'three times the normal size'. Her accommodation aft for the master and mates was very well fitted out indeed, with oak and larch panelling and she had central heating in her after accommodation. The master's night cabin had a four-poster bed and he had his own bathroom. Foreward was a saloon with the stewards' berth leading off it and on the opposite side of the vessel a spare cabin for occasional passengers, who would usually be shareholders in the vessel. Forward of an athwartships bulkhead was a mess room which the mates and carpenter shared with the central heating boiler. The mates' berths were in small cabins to the port side of the messroom.

The deckhouse forecastle had berths for six men and a bosun's locker. Also in this deckhouse was the donkey, a utility American Buffalo winch engine. The vessel was, of course, entirely dependent on this engine for the hoisting of the sails and the anchors and sometimes for working cargo. In many big schooners, the steam donkey or motor winch was also used to work the pumps but, even at the end of her life, according to Captain Karl V Karlsson, the *Bertha L. Downs* leaked very little and there was seldom occasion to use the motor for this purpose.

When the *Bertha L. Downs* was launched a local newspaper, the *Bath Anvil* for 18 January 1908, published an account of the occasion which conveys something of the atmosphere surrounding her building and the society that commissioned her construction.

> The first in Bath in 1908 and the first vessel to be launched from the yard of the New England Co. for two years went down the ways Thursday (Jan. 16) morning, a veritable triumph of the modern shipbuilders' skill.
>
> The schooner was the *Bertha L. Downs*, built by Hon. E.W. Hyde for the Benedict-Manson Co. of New Haven, Conn., to be added to their large fleet of coastwise vessels.
>
> In spite of the lowering skies and the slight rain of the morning, a large crowd gathered at this famous yard to see the schooner take her maiden dip into the blue waters of the Kennebec.
>
> The launching was scheduled for 10.30 and it was just five minutes past the allotted time when the cry went up, 'she moves', and the craft slipped easily and gracefully down the ways. As the vessel went into the Kennebec, Miss Bertha L. Downs of New Haven, Conn., the sponsor of the craft and the young lady for whom she is named, christened her with a magnificent bouquet of roses and gracefully waved the United States flag. The whistles along the waterfront tooted and signalled to the waiting city that another maritime triumph had been added to Bath's long list.
>
> On board the craft with Miss Downs as members of the launching party were Capt. and Mrs. E.H. Weaver, J. W. Haskell and Miss Villa Haskell, Miss Corey and M.B. Hemmingway of New Haven, Capt. Robert F. Wells of Stony Brook, L.I., who is to command the *Downs*, Capt.

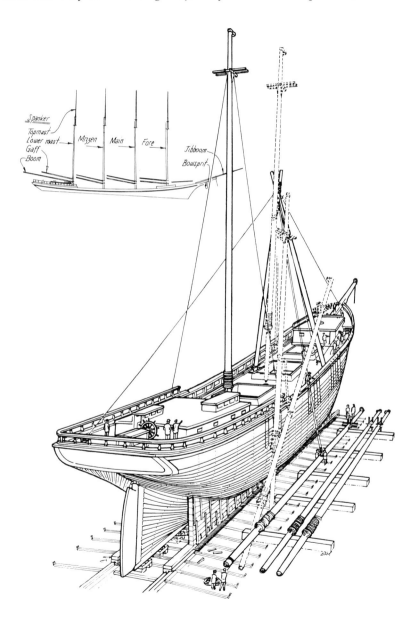

Stepping the masts of the Bertha L. Downs. *The spanker mast has been stepped and partly stayed and the sheers, made up from salvaged spars, has been moved forward to hoist the mizzen.*

F.C. Crosseley of New Haven, who is to go in command of the duplicate of the *Downs* which Mr. Hyde is building at the New England yard, and Rev. and Mrs. Culbert McGay of this city. Many prominent Bath citizens and mariners of note witnessed the launching of the craft from points of vantage on shore.

The *Downs* swung easily into the stream where she was anchored and then brought back to the wharf and the launching party disembarked, going to Mr. Hyde's home on High Street where a very enjoyable buffet luncheon was served in honour of this event.

The party here were joined by Senator Harold M. Sewell, Treas. and Mrs. I.S. Coombs of the New England Co., Mrs. W.S. Glidden, Sheriff John W. Ballou, N. Gratz Jackson, Capt. J.W. Hawley and others. A tempting menu of lobster salad, sandwiches, coffee and ices was served and many impromptu speeches were made in honour of the event.

Both Capt. Weaver who is a director of the Benedict-Manson Co. and Capt. Wells, who is the commander of the new craft, expressed themselves in unmistakable terms as to their satisfaction with the new vessel. Capt. Wells is very proud of her and says that he never saw a better built or finer equipped craft.

The *Downs* is a duplicate of the *William J. Quillin,* built by the New England Co. in 1905, which has made one of the best records for speed and carrying. She is 716 gross tons, 175.4 feet long, 37.1 feet breadth, 14.2 feet deep, and will have a carrying capacity of 1200 tons of coal and 600,000 feet of lumber. The frame is hard wood, bottom, oak, and top Michigan hackmatack. The decks are of white pine with composition fastening and in every particular the best of material is used throughout her construction. She is single-decked and is intended for the general carrying trade. She has all the modern conveniences for handling a cargo, including a 12-horsepower gasolene hoisting engine, a Hyde windlass and patent riding stoppers. The masts are of Oregon pine, 92 feet long, the fore being 26 inches in diameter and the others being 25 inches. The rigging is wire set up with turnbuckles, and she will spread 5000 yards of canvas. She carries two small boats, the larger being 22 feet long and equipped with a 4 H.P. gasolene engine, one of the first launches ever provided for a vessel in this city. The other is 16 feet in length. Both boats were built by the Bath Auto and Gas Engine Co. of this city.

All the iron work about the decks is galvanized and the *Downs* carries two Baldt stockless anchors of the most improved style, weighing 4070 and 4090 pounds and attached to 1⅞ chains.

The cabins of the craft are finished in quartered oak and are fitted with every convenience of latter day shipbuilding. They are heated by the hot water system and are ornaments to the splendid craft.

The *Downs* is rated A1 for 15 years and launched ready for sea. She is expected to leave this port today for Philadelphia to load for New Haven and has shipped a crew of eight men.

Capt. Robert F. Wells, her commander, although one of the youngest captains in the coastwise service, is considered one of the best and is one of the best appearing young men that Bath has seen for a long time. He has been here for some time getting his craft ready for the launching and while here has made a host of friends who extent to him congratulations on his good fortune in getting so fine a craft and their best wishes for success with her. His former commands have been the schrs. *Clifford N. Carver* and *George W. Wells.*

The men who are directly responsible for the building of the craft, by that we mean the men who actually worked with their hands upon her construction and who in the past have helped to make Bath's name famous as the finest shipbuilding city in the world, are Horatio N. Douglass, master workman in charge of construction; master joiner, Frank N. Haggett; master fastener, George Lightbody; master blacksmith, Hiram Pattee; master painter, James Wheeler; rigger, Capt. Robert H. Goodman; sailmaker, A.M. Cutler; planker, H.E. Worrey; caulker, Tibbetts and Oliver; sparmaker, Frank Parris.

The members of the launching party from New Haven returned to their homes on the afternoon train, greatly pleased with their visit to Bath. They all say that they will be sure to come down to the launching of schooner No. 2 for the Benedict-Manson Co. which will be a duplicate of the *Downs* and which is expected to be ready for launching about the first of April.

The *Downs* presented a pretty picture in the stream Thursday, gaily bedecked with signal flags. She is almost a yacht in her graceful lines and splendid construction, and well may her captain feel proud of being the commander of such a vessel.

This is Hon. E.W. Hyde's first venture into the wooden shipbuilding field, although as president of the Iron Works he has a long list of steel vessels to his credit. The approximate cost of the *Downs* is $55,000 and as one of the sailors in the crew said yesterday after a tour of inspection, 'she's worth every cent of it and some more'.

The life of the *Bertha L. Downs*

The Benedict-Manson Marine Company, for which concern the *Bertha L. Downs* was built, had been formed in 1906 as the successors to the firm of Benedict and Downs, founded in 1890 from an earlier partnership established in 1877 'to do a wholesale business in coal'. These companies were themselves successors to an earlier coal marketing concern, H.W. Benedict & Son.[37] Each of these companies had been shipowners — principally of schooners — as well as coal factors. When Benedict Downs and Co was formed in April 1890 they announced from their address in New Haven, Connecticut,

> We beg to announce that we shall continue to sell, all rail via New York and New England R.R. and central New England and Wester R.R. (Poughkeepsie Bridge Route) and connections, and by boat, the same anthracite, bituminous and gas coals as have been handled by Benedict and Downs, and by a strict attention to the wants of the trade, we hope to merit a large share of your patronage.
>
> All orders by mail, telegraph, or long-distance shall have prompt attention.

The business and shipowning structure of the Benedict-Manson Marine Company's operations was not dissimilar to that of William F Palmer, which have already been described. It was an association of vessels, with many individual shareholders in each vessel brought together under managing shareholders at a time when competition in the coal trade was becoming more intense. Altogether some 27 schooners, three- and four-masters, were managed at one time or another by the Benedict-Manson Company.

The history of the Benedict-Downs Manson Companies is, in fact, a microcosm of the history of the big United States schooners as it has been presented here in general terms. The fleet prospered at first but, after the collapse of the Virginia coal trade for schooners in 1909 it had varied fortunes. In 1909 the group comprised 22 schooners of capacity of from 250 tons of coal to 2100 tons. A new schooner was ordered from builders at Rockland, Maine, and the management was moderately optimistic as to the prospects.

By 1912 crisis had set in. Management reported to stockholders,

> When this company was organised in February, 1906, there seemed every reason to believe that it would have a prosperous future, but in 1907 the financial panic came on, since which time business of all kinds has been depressed and shipping has suffered as much, if not more, than other lines.
>
> In addition a revolution in coast transportation has taken place — steamers are being introduced in the coal carrying trade and taking business at such rates that your directors would not advise the investment of any further capital to compete. Meanwhile our vessels are finding employment to a considerable extent in the timber trade at satisfactory rates with fairly good prospects for some months.

Such was the direct and immediate effect of the construction of the tidewater piers served by the Virginia railway at Norfolk in 1909. The era of the schooner was coming to an end. The Benedict-Manson Company made a loss in 1912 and underwent capital restructuring. During these years, registered at New Haven, Connecticut, as managed by the Benedict-Manson Marine Company, the *Bertha L. Downs* worked principally, like the rest of the fleet, in the lumber and coal trades from the southern ports of the United States to New England ports. It was during this period of her existence that the frontispiece photograph was taken.

The Benedict-Manson Marine Company, like many other schooner owners in the United States, was saved by the First World War boom and was able to sell itself, very profitably, out of existence. In 1915 tonnage values began to rise very steeply and the directors decided to dispose of the fleet while it was profitable to do so. The decision to sell was first announced in a notice to stockholders on 31 March 1916, which read, in part,

> The demand for tonnage has been so unprecedented that it has seemed to your Board of Directors an opportune time to dispose of some or all of the vessels comprising the fleet if satisfactory prices could be obtained, and in pursuance of that policy the company's holdings in two vessels have been sold . . . and negotiations are now pending for the sale of two or three more.

The schooners were then steadily sold off and while the process was going on, on 13 December 1916, the stockholders voted that the corporate existence of the Benedict-Manson Marine Company should be terminated. The *Bertha L. Downs* was advertised as of:

> . . . four masts, single deck, 606 net, 716 tons gross register, dimensions 175.4 × 37.1 × 14.2, carries approximately 1,100 tons of coal or 575 M feet of yellow pine lumber on draft of 17'. Now bound to Para, Brazil and

proceeds from there to Jamaica to load logwood for a US port north of Hatteras. Price $100,000.

The Benedict-Manson Marine Company, having disposed of all their vessels, paid their final dividend in March 1919.

It will be remembered that the *Bertha L. Downs* had cost approximately $55,000 to build in 1908. In 1916 the Benedict-Manson Marine Company disposed of her to her Master, Captain Robert F Wells for $80,000. Captain Wells had been her Master since her launch. He came from Long Island and was master of the four-master *Clifford N. Carver* by the time he was twenty-five. He was invariably successful, highly regarded by his fellow shipmasters and an excellent businessman. He told W J Lewis Parker when the latter interviewed him in the early 1950s that he felt very strongly that the Benedict-Manson Marine Company should have held on to their vessels for rather longer against a further rise in tonnage values. He, and perhaps one or two of his friends, were reputed to have made a lot of money buying and selling schooners in 1916 and 1917. After the War he was able to set himself up with an automobile selling business in his home town of Port Jefferson, and he prospered handsomely in this further venture.

Captain Wells registered the *Bertha L. Downs* as the property of the 'Bertha L. Downs Shipping Corporation' of New York. The New York maritime register notes for 29 November 1916 report the charter of the *Bertha L. Downs*, New York to Copenhagen, oil cake, private terms, prompt. The pre-paid freight for this charter may have been as much as $75,000, given the rates running at the time. The *Bertha L. Downs* sailed from New York on 24 December 1916 for Aarhus under the command of Captain Sørensen and she arrived at Lerwick, Shetland, on 25 January 1917, sailed on 10 February and arrived at Aarhus on 17 February. The last report shows her arriving at Aalborg on 28 February.

In February 1917 a Presidential Proclamation declared a 'a national emergency arising from insufficiency of maritime tonnage . . .' and prohibited the sale of American vessels to foreigners under authority of the US Shipping Board Act. When the *Bertha L. Downs* had sailed from New York the United States was a neutral in the First World War. She sailed under the American flag with her name and nationality and the American flag conspicuously displayed on her sides. She was sailing from one neutral country to another. The photograph on page 45 shows her lying fully laden in a Danish port shortly after her arrival in Scandinavian waters. The United States declared war on Germany on 6 April 1917 and shortly afterwards the regulation forbidding the sale of American tonnage to foreigners was relaxed in relation to sailing vessels already in European waters because it was considered too risky to bring them home. Meanwhile, the prices owners were ready to pay for ships continued to rise in Europe as well as in North America and the *Bertha L. Downs*, now to be re-named *Atlas*, was sold to a group of four Copenhagen shareholders registered as the Atlas Company and given Danish registry on 24 December 1917. In February next year the ownership was formally transferred to the Rederi-A/S Trans (R A Robbert) and registered at Copenhagen as the *Atlas* under the command of Captain H Nielsen. The sum involved is not known but in 1917 the sale price to a neutral country for a four-masted schooner of the class of the *Atlas* is likely to have been very high and it is probable that her new owners were able to employ her profitably for two or three years before the great shipping slump which followed closely upon the end of the First World War. From 1920 onwards however, she would have depreciated very rapidly in value and may well have been laid up, together with a number of Danish four-masters, including brand new vessels, the building of which had started during the boom period but which found no employment after their launch.

R A Robbert was one of the original four shareholders. He was also the managing owner of the steamer *Hamlet* of 1150 tons, built in 1890, the three-masted schooner *Skandia*, 150 tons, built in 1902, and he was shortly to acquire the new steamer *Aladdin*, built in 1919, 1038 tons.[38] These steamers may have enabled the company to survive, but with the onset of the worldwide surplus of tonnage in 1921, it certainly must have caught a cold with the *Atlas*. On the 24 May 1923 she was registered as of the Port of Mariehamn in the Åland Islands of Finland[39] having been sold to Arthur Andersson of Mariehamn and fellow shareholders for 25,500 Danish Crowns a sum which at the time may have represented about $10,000 at the most — perhaps £2,500.[40]

At her initial Finnish registration the managing owner was shown in Mariehamn's Ships Register as Captain Arthur Ekbom with 5 $\frac{1}{100}$ths shares in the vessel. Captain Arthur Andersson, also of Mariehamn, became the managing owner in November 1927. Throughout her years under the Finnish flag Captain Arthur Andersson was the principal shareholder with 52 $\frac{1}{100}$ths. His Åland partners were three sea captains and two ladies of Mariehamn who each had 5 $\frac{1}{100}$ths shares. But the second principal shareholder, holding the remaining 18 $\frac{1}{100}$ths, is described in the ship register as 'Handl. Percy Appleby, Nystad'. Percy Appleby was, in fact, a well-known London shipbroker whose principal business lay with Baltic timber trade vessels. Through the years he held varying numbers of shares in many Åland vessels, principally the old steamships which began to be acquired after 1928. The *Atlas* during her period of Finnish registration was therefore essentially an Anglo–Finnish venture and it is not surprising that she was regularly employed in the timber trade to London. Appleby was a Swedish speaker and a frequent visitor to Mariehamn. He and his fellow shareholders had probably acquired the *Atlas* at a bargain price.

In 1927 Captain Karl V Karlsson of Wårdö was appointed a master of the *Atlas*, and in May 1928 he acquired 5 $\frac{1}{100}$ths shares in her. Under Karl Karlsson's command *Atlas* became a regular visitor to the Regent's Canal Dock in London, where she discharged her sweet-smelling timber cargoes from the Gulf of Bothnia ports. She brought two cargoes a year into London and made two trips to Denmark from the northern Baltic, one to Kolding and one to Copenhagen. She was, of course, laid up each winter when the northern Baltic froze over. Karl Karlsson told me in the early 1980s that he had taken pride in tacking her among the ice flows of the northern Baltic when he sailed north to load the first cargo of the season.

These lumber cargoes were loaded at Swedish ports on the west coast of the Gulf of Bothnia. The *Atlas* lay out in the roadsteads at anchor an the lumber was brought out alongside her in barges and stowed by gang of women stevedors, called 'splitvedjäntor', which could be translate 'lathwood lasses'. The timber was the offcuts of the local sawmills, from 18in to 6ft long: boards and battens, mostly pine, used in Britain an western Europe for a number of different purposes, such as furnitur making, the making of fruit boxes, fish boxes and crates, for fencing, fo the paving of roads in those days of horses, and the small, damaged, stuf for firewood. It was loaded into the *Atlas* with the old American o engine (which Karl Karlsson described as 'a son of a bitch') working th cargo gaffs. Up to 40 women handled the cargo, many of them, from surviving photographs, young and pretty, and they were very quick t sort out the material which had been thrown higgledy-piggledy into th barges and to stow it both in the hold and in deck cargo, though it wa killing work. The crew worked the winches and cargo gaffs, but the never touched the lumber. There was a strong social convention unde which they never touched the women either.

Captain Karlsson found the *Atlas* very handy, especially when loadec She sailed very well indeed, though it was difficult to get her to com round through the wind when she was in ballast. She sailed at her bes with the draft of 17ft 6in forward and 17ft aft, which was a bit deep for th Baltic trades. Captain Karlsson was impressed with the fact that she had 20-ton fresh water tank — most vessels in the Baltic trade had only 1 to of fresh water on board. And he was impressed also with the beautifu oak, birch, and larch panelling of the after accommodation. The *Atlas* als still had her central heating, aft, an unheard-of luxury in an Åland Island vessel.

Such was the power of the *Atlas* under sail that the gaff topsails hac only very rarely to be taken in on Baltic passages. The same crew o eleven Ålanders (including the master and mates) joined her year afte year and got to know her so well that she could be put round, laden, i nine minutes from start to finish. The years spent in command of this fin vessel were very happy ones for Captain Karlsson and on some of hi passages he was accompanied by his wife and elder son (who later be came head of the Åland Ministry of Education). It is not surprising that h treasured a splendid model of her made by the late Viktor Andersson, a famous Åland craftsman.

In 1931 during the winter lay-up, the shareholding group having inves ted in steam tonnage, the *Atlas* was sold to Harald Kjaer, a timber mer chant of Copenhagen, and to Estonian partners of whom the principa was Captain Kristian Jurnas of Pärnu in Estonia. The *Atlas*' registratio was transferred to Pärnu and she sailed under the Estonian flag unde Captain Jurnas' managing ownership but with partly Danish crews. I 1949 I crossed the Skagerrak from Hirtshals to Kristiansand in a Danisl ferry, the mate of which had served in *Atlas*. A year later Kristian Jurnas who was recently described to me by Urmas Dresen of the Estonia Maritime Museum at Tallin as 'a real hard case', became managing owne of the *Gunn*, bought from Åland owners who had purchased her from th Norwegian partnership in 1925. In 1934 he and his partners bought th *Josiah B. Chase* built at Boothbay, Maine, in 1921 and the last four-maste o be launched in the State, which he re-named *Mihkel*, and the *James C. Hamlen* launched at Portland, Maine, in 1920, which he re-named *Jaan*. Under his management also was the *Clara Davis*, built at Mystic, Connecticut, in 1905, which was re-named *Martha*. There was thus a fleet of at least five United States-built four-masters trading in North European waters in the 1930s.

When the country gained its independence from Russia at the end of the First World War Estonian shipping was predominantly in sailing tonnage and it was only slowly that a transition to power-driven vessels took place between the two world wars. Many wooden sailing vessels were built in Estonia in the 1920s, partly because there was a strong sailing tradition and partly because seafaring tended to be a business conducted by small family concerns with very small capital. The story of the development of Estonian shipping until the Second World War is complex and some account of it has been given in two papers by Knut Berg and Jaak Sammet.[41]

By the 1930s the bulk of the Estonian merchant ship fleet comprised old steamers, and Captain Jurnas' managing ownership of large four-masted schooners was something of an anomaly. Berg comments (p156),

> One can ask why Estonia stuck to the relatively large schooners, which were, in the thirties, universally considered as obsolete, but the answer will be hard to find. It would have been easier to understand if it had been a continuation of the traditional trading with home-built ships, but the American-built schooners were, in the first place, much larger than the Baltic-built ones. They were also mostly acquired after the wooden shipbuilding had actually ceased on the coast of Estonia.

Berg comments that the Jurnas schooners plus the training barquentine *Tormilind* comprised more than one half of Estonia's sailing ship tonnage in the later 1930s. Further research in Estonia into this intriguing question is clearly necessary, but a possible answer rests in the working relationship Captain Jurnas appears to have had with Harald Kjaer, the Danish timber merchant for whom his schooners provided a steady flow of timber cargoes from the Gulf of Bothnia. The vessels purchased in America which had previously been laid up in Boothbay Harbour and Eastport, Maine, had been acquired at rock-bottom prices complete with sails and gear. They could make an average of four Baltic and North Sea round voyages each summer sailing season when the Gulf of Bothnia ports were not frozen over and as long as they required neither expensive repairs nor much new gear, crew costs being minimal, they could make a reasonable return on the capital invested in them. Certainly the successful operation of these big schooners attracted a good deal of attention in the shipping world of the later 1930s. It was at this period that Michal Leszczynski, the Polish Master Mariner artist, who was at this time himself sailing in the Gulf of Bothnia timber trade, made a number of very attractive pencil drawings of these vessels, some of which were published in England. Michal Leszczynski as a wartime refugee later became master of the British ketch *Garlandstone* in the trade from the Bristol Channel to Ireland.[42]

The international interest in these vessels arose partly from the fact that they were not confined to the Baltic but from time to time discharged cargoes in London, as did the *Jaan* as late as January 1938. She cleared again for London from Hernosand in Sweden on 9 August 1939. Whether she completed the passage (Britain declared war on Germany on 3 September 1939) is not known, but she certainly returned to Copenhagen where she was laid up next year.

In the 1930s Captain Daniel R Bolt published monthly reports of the movements of merchant sailing vessels in the Baltic and other trades in the house magazine of the Pacific Steam Navigation Company, *Sea Breezes*. These reports were based on movements culled from Lloyds' list and also on correspondence with friends in Copenhagen, North America, and elsewhere. Although they were never complete, it is easy to follow through them the movements of the *Gunn* and the *Jaan*. Both are shown to be constantly busy in the Baltic trade with an occasional passage to London until the outbreak of war in Europe, when censorship brought the reports to an end. Oddly enough the *Atlas* is never mentioned, nor are *Mihkel* or *Martha*, though from the fact that she went aground off Nystad in southern Sweden in November 1937, when deep-laden with lumber for Copenhagen, and was subsequently broken up, it is apparent that the latter vessel was currently employed in the same trade.

A letter from Sven Tvermoes of Copenhagen in *Sea Breezes* of May 1938 which describes the breaking up of *Martha* records that the *Atlas*, *Gunn* and *Jaan* were all in Copenhagen in the spring of 1938 having brought wood cargoes 'and have been here the whole winter'.

The *Atlas*, the *Jaan* and the *Mihkel* were all laid up in Copenhagen in August 1940, after the Russians had occupied Estonia.[43] *Gunn* had been destroyed by fire in Copenhagen in January 1940.[44]

The Baltic was extensively mined and sailing vessels, unable to keep to the narrow cleared channels, were prevented from operating in these waters. It was to be some time after the War before the magnetic and acoustic mines were either cleared or considered harmless. Indeed, it was 1970 before all the mines were declared safe. Nevertheless, the Finnish four-masted schooner *Yxpila* of Raumo, under Captain Lasse Andersson did sail in the Baltic with timber cargoes during the summers of 1942 and 1943, despite the dangers from the mines and from both Russian and German submarines.[45]

Captain Søren Thirslund, formerly in the Danish Greenland trade and from the early 1980s a staff member of the Danish National Maritime Museum at Helsingør remembers the *Atlas* lying in Copenhagen until late 1943. He was, in those years of the German occupation of Denmark, making a little money, while studying for his mate's and master's certificates of competence, by acting as weekend watchman on board the laid-up motorship *Dana*. Immediately astern of her in the Sydhaven of Copenhagen lay the *Atlas* and young Thirslund used to pull round her in one of *Dana*'s boats, noting that she was 'very long-haired in the bottom' and still bore the port of registry, Pärnu, on her transom counter. What happened to *Mihkel* is not known, but after August 1943, probably in October that year, the *Atlas* and the *Jaan* were taken over by the occupying German authorities and towed to Kiel. Here the *Jaan* was damaged by Allied bombing, but the *Atlas* survived and, being a very strongly-built vessel, was in good enough order to be used as an engine repair vessel in

1946–47.[46] She appears later to have been towed to the Elbe and given the German name *Prinzessin Alice*. Here she was used as an accommodation vessel.

The wreck of the *Jaan* was partly broken up near Kiel for fuel during the bad European winter of 1946–47 but substantial remains of her were visible on the beach for thirty or more years after. The *Atlas* was sold in 1950 and broken up at Wewelsfleth near Hamburg (which cannot be identified in *The Times Atlas of the World*) after forty-two years of work under five flags.

Appendix

Ray Buck, Bristol Channel Pilot, of Pill, Somerset, has provided the following delightful impression of an Englishman's brief view of a big American schooner in 1937.

> The third time we were sent to Barry to spend one tide looking for a Yank schooner bound for Newport. It was November, fog coming down and clearing. No radar in those days. Ship bells ringing whilst they prudently remained at anchor, blasts of whistles and syrens and an occasional honk from an Appledore ketch's hand operated fog horn, the 'bay' of the different lightships (all those years after I can still reproduce the two-toned boom of the English and Welsh), the more Drake-minded mariners under way. Fog in busy shipping lanes always seemed to produce its own peculiar cacophonous sound. A mournful discord in keeping with the weather about. High water we took a sweep out to the Fathom Bank and then proceeded up between the Holms in sometimes thick fog. On coming near the lightship and interlaced with its time-patterned baying we were amazed to hear the sound of a banjo playing negro music, dead slow and approaching the direction we hit a clear patch. There about two cables from the lightship anchored snugly was our quarry, the five-masted schooner *Edna Hoyt*, her stern revealing her Port of Register as Savannah, U.S.A. and just forward of her jigger mast a venerable old gentleman was sat in a wicker chair (turned out to be the Captain) playing the banjo surrounded by Negros sat down in various attitudes of repose singing. What an absolutely amazing sight.

The *Edna Hoyt* was built at Thomaston, Maine, in 1920 and was the last five-master to be launched. Unlike most of her wartime and postwar-built sisters, after a slow start she had a highly successful career, being constantly employed through the 1920s and 1930s. In the summer of 1937 she took timber from Halifax, Nova Scotia, to Belfast, Northern Ireland, and then sailed light to Newport, South Wales, where she loaded Welsh coal for Venezuela. She was damaged by bad weather in the Bay of Biscay and condemned after being forced into Lisbon. She was the last of the American five-masters at sea.

Her master, the 'venerable old gentleman' was Captain George Hopkins. He was frequently accompanied to sea by his wife — see Tod, *The Last of Sail Down East*, Barre, Mass., 1965, pp10–13.

Notes

1 As in Des Barres, *Surveys of North America, entitled 'Atlantic Neptune'; published by command of government for the use of the Royal Navy of Great Britain*, London, W Babbs, 1781.

2 H I Chapelle, *The History of American Sailing Ships*, New York 1935, pp219–220.

3 For a good account of the development of the use of the schooner rig in British waters see Starkey, *The British Schooner in the Nineteenth Century*, in the volume entitled *Sail's Last Century* in *Conway's History of the Ship*, London 1993.

4 It is to be borne in mind that the word 'schooner', without qualification, was used to describe a two-masted vessel. If she had three or more masts she was describd as a three-masted or four-masted schooner. The expression 'two-masted schooner' was not normally used in the years when schooners were commonplace since it was a tautology, as was, incidentally, 'three-masted barque', a term used by sea writers but not by seamen. It had, of course, no significance until the development of the four-masted barque in the 1880s at the very end of the history of the sailing vessel.

5 For a comprehensive account of the British merchant schooner and her world at this period see Greenhill, *The Merchant Schooners*, 4th, revised edition, London 1988. For two firsthand accounts of the realities of schooner operations see Slade, *Out of Appledore*, London 1980, and Eglinton, *The Last of the Sailing Coasters*, London 1982.

6 For a thorough study of British coasting ketches in the late nineteenth and twentieth centuries see Slade & Greenhill, *West Country Coasting Ketches*, London 1974. For a detailed account of the seamanship of handling a ketch see Eglinton, *The 'Mary Fletcher'*, Exeter 1990.

7 The *Empire* was bought by owners in Wicklow, Ireland, in 1876 and registered at Liverpool as a schooner. She was bought by owners in Appledore, Devon, in 1886 after stranding in the Bristol Channel and re-rigged as a ketch, retaining her schooner's foremast as her main. She was employed in the local coasting trade until her loss in 1913, see Slade and Greenhill, *op. cit.* p58. The *Empire* may have been one of the small two-masters, usually of fisherman design, from New England, which until the late 1880s made annual voyages to England with cargoes of apples packed in barrels. Certainly she looks like a sharpshooter fisherman in an early twentieth-century photograph. See W Bunting, *Portrait of a Port, Boston, 1852–1914*, Harvard University Press 1971, p222, and B B Crowninshield, *Fore and Afters*, Boston 1940, p33.

8 Bunting, *Steamers, Schooners, Cutters & Sloops*, Boston 1974, p116.

9 The classic book on the fishing schooner is Chapelle, *The American Fishing Schooners 1825–1935*, New York 1973. Among numerous other books on the New England fishery see especially Berman, *Down on T Wharf*, Mystic, Conn. 1982, which contains a vast amount of background information.

10 See Parker, *The Great Coal Schooners of New England*, The Marine Historical Association, Mystic, Conn. 1948. See also his chapter in *Sail's Last Century*, a volume of *Conway's History of the Ship*; and numerous articles and papers in various journals and published collections including *Down East*, a magazine published in Camden, Maine, and the Belfast (Maine) *Courier-Gazette*.

11 *The Governor Ames, as She Was and As She Should Be* by R B Forbes, published by James F Cotter & Co., Printers, apparently in 1889, place not stated. See also Forbes, *Personal Reminiscences*, Boston 1882.

12 In *Down East Magazine* for July, 1970

13 In *The National Fisherman* for February, 1975

14 In a private communication.

15 Rowland, *About the Big Coasters*, in Smith, *Workaday Schooners*, Camden, Maine, 1975, pp. 176–7.

16 Hughes, *Through Mighty Seas*, London, No date given, p77.

17 In a private communication.

18 Bunting, *op. cit.*, p40.

19 For an account of the importance and use of 'sail assist' in operating early steam vessels see the chapter entitled *Sail Assist and the Early Steamship* by Allington and Greenhill in the volume *The Advent of Steam* in *Conway's History of the Ship*. See also Greenhill and Allington, 'The SS Great Britain as the World's First Six-Masted Schooner' in *Maritime Wales No 9*, Caernarvon, 1985, and Greenhill and Giffard, *Steam, Politics & Patronage. The Transformation of the Royal Navy, 1815–54*, London 1994.

20 Safford, *The Decline of the American Merchant Marine, 1850–1914: An Historiographic Appraisal*, in Fischer & Panting eds. *Change and Adaptation in Maritime History, The North Atlantic Fleets in the Nineteenth Century*, St. Johns, Newfoundland, 1985.

21 W J Lewis Parker, 'The Operation and Management of the Great New England Schooners 1870–1900' in *Problems of Ship Management and Operation 1870–1900* London, 1972, p17.

22 W J Lewis Parker, *William F Palmer and the Palmer Fleet*, unpublished lecture dated Camden, Maine, 23 April 1984 and delivered at the Maine Maritime Museum at Bath, Maine in early May 1984.

23 W J Lewis Parker, *The Gov. Ames, Maine's First Five-Masted Schooner* in *Down East*, Camden, Maine, July 1979, p49.

24 Charles S Morgan, *Coastal Shipping Under Sail, 1880–1920*, The Newcomen Society in North America 1979.

25 Paul C. Morris, *Four-Masted Schooners of the East Coast*, Orleans, Massachusetts, 1975, p5.

26 The history of William F Palmer and his schooner-owning operations is dealt with in detail in W J Lewis Parker's unpublished lecture, see footnote 22 above.

27 Charles Morgan, *op. cit.*

28 Greenhill, *Karlsson: The Life of an Åland Seafarer*, London 1982, p24.

29 Francis E Bowker, *Herbert L. Rawding*, Mystic, Conn. 1986, p79. Giles M Tod, *The Last Sail Down East*, Barre, Mass. 1965, p90–91.

30 John Parker, *Sails of the Maritimes*, Sydney, N.S. 1960, p168.

31 *The Western Morning News*, 17 July 1901.

32 *Lostwithiel and Fowey Guardian*, 26 July 1901.

33 The *Boston Journal*, 17 October 1901.

34 Oral communication from W J Lewis Parker.

35 Figure from Morris, *op. cit.*, p7 and 14, and a private communication from W J Lewis Parker. A very scholarly and comprehensive account of the building of schooners on the Kennebec, together with a great deal about the vessels themselves and their operation, is to be found in the late William A Baker's masterly *'A Maritime History of Bath, Maine'*, Bath, 1973, 2 vols.

36 Greenhill and Manning, *The Evolution of the Wooden Ship*, London and New York 1988, pp91–98.

37 All information about the Benedict-Manson Marine Co., its predecessors and its activities, is taken from an unpublished typescript 'Magnus Manson and the Benedict-Manson Marine Co.' written by Harry Sherman Holcomb, a descendant of the Manson family. This typescript was most kindly made available to the authors by Mr Holcomb's son, Dr Harry S Holcomb III, of Franktown, Virginia.

38 Det Norske Veritas, Register over Skandinaviske Skibe, Kristiania (Oslo) 1920.

39 Ålands Ships Register.

40 Holm-Petersen, *Danske firmastskonnerter*, Marstal, Denmark, 1989, p20; and Georg and Karl Kåhre, *Den åländska segelsjöfartens historia*, Mariehamn, 1988, p547.

41 Knut Berg, *Baltic Shipping* in *Sjöfartshistorisk Årbok, 1975*, Bergen, Norway, 1976, pp121–198, and Jaak Sammet, *Steamboats and Sailing Vessels in Estonia in the 1920s* in *The Baltic as a Trade Road*, publication number 16 in the series of the Provincial Museum of Kymenlaakso, Finland, 1990, pp204–224.

42 See Leszczynski, *How to Draw Sail and Sea*, London, 1944, pp46, 49, 53, 54–57. The commercial succes of these vessels is perhaps indicated by the fact that the four-master *Josephine A. McQuesten* built at Rockland, Maine in 1920 was bought by Captain Jurnas as late as 1936 but was lost on her delivery passage.

43 Information from Frederik Fredericksen, Copenhagen, via Captain Søren Thirslund of that city.

44 Berg, *op. cit.*, p186.

45 Letter from Captain Karl Kåhre, Mariehamn, December 1991.

46 The account of the last years of *Atlas* comes from Fredericksen.

The Graphics

The *Bertha L. Downs* and her sistership, *Mary Manson Gruener*, were built by rule of thumb to a stated length of keel, a stated breadth of so many feet, and to a stated carrying capacity of so many tons. There were no builder's plans as we know them today. The master builder may have begun with moulds for frame pieces sent down by the vessel's modeller or designer, or he may have borrowed moulds from another yard to duplicate a specific vessel. He may also have begun with hull offsets – measurements — taken from a half model and recorded in a loftsman's notebook. With these offsets he would lay down the heights and breadths required to build the moulds. No documentation exists which pinpoints the origin of these two vessels: neither marked moulds, loftsman's notes or a half model relating to the *Downs* and the *Gruener* have been found.

It is possible that both these four-masted schooners of 1908 were built to offsets taken from a model carved for the *William J. Quillin*, a similar and successful schooner built on the same location three years earlier, as noted in the *Bath Anvil*'s account of the *Downs*' launching, 18 January 1908. If so, her modeller was named as Frederick W Rideout in the *Bath Times*' coverage of the *Quillin*'s launch on the earlier occasion. Frederick W Rideout, Johnson Rideout II (his father) and William Pattee were master shipwrights and ship modellers who separately or together had modelled, designed or made the frame moulds for most of the commercial vessels built at Bath, Maine, from the late 1860s to the opening decade of the 1900s.

Whatever her likeness to the *William J. Quillin* might be, it is quite possible that the model, moulds or offsets for the *Bertha L. Downs* came from another source. John J Wardwell, NA, of nearby Rockland, Maine held equal stature as designer and modeller in the development of fine-lined, multi-masted schooners for the coal, ice and hard pine trades. Captain Douglas K Lee, schooner historian and present-day builder, owner and operator of windjammer schooners at Rockland, points out that J J Wardwell had modelled and supervised construction of the schooner *Dean E. Brown* at the Cobb-Butler shipyard, Rockland, during 1907. The *Brown* was the first of four similar schooners contracted for by the Benedict-Manson Marine Company of New Haven, Connecticut. Two more of the Benedict-Manson schooners, the *Bertha L. Downs* and the *Mary Manson Gruener* were built at Bath the following year in a temporary location by an irregular crew. The site was leased land in the defunct New England Company shipyard. The builder was Edward W Hyde, president of the Bath Iron Works. Horatio N Douglass, master carpenter, oversaw the actual construction.

So, lacking construction plans, half model, or even recorded offsets attributed to the four-masted schooner *Bertha L. Downs* of 1908, how do we draw accurate graphics to explore her hull structure? Well, several things are known. First, she was of a fairly common type, judging from her surviving photographs: a single-decked, four-masted schooner intended for the coal, pilings and hard pine trades, with hull shape and deck furniture quite similar to that seen in photographs of other four-masted schooners built in many locations along the US Atlantic coast at that time.

Second, the hull survey exists which established her underwriters' classification at the time of her launch in January 1908. The survey lists her registered measurements, her timber scantlings, her spars, sails and her mechanical equipment. This schooner was given a high rating, 1-A for fifteen years, which means that she was built under inspection to a rigid set of rules, and that she was given the best of everything including cross-strapping of the hull with iron.

Third, the rules governing insurable ship structure are published by the underwriters' classification societies, notably, for most Bath-built vessels, the American Bureau of Shipping. Take a given set of hull lines, apply wood and iron to them in the manner specified by these ABS Rules, and you'll have a vessel suitable for A-1 classification. Hyde and Douglass did it with timber back in 1908. We can do it on paper in 1993. The plane and perspective drawings which follow do not attempt to freeze and document the *Bertha L. Downs per se*. Rather, they intend to portray a four-masted schooner of her general dimensions and character that works, can be modelled, and even built at full size if you wish to do it.

There is still another source of information for drawing this hull accurately. It is the source that we will mainly follow here. Builders' plans for a four-masted schooner of this character were drawn up in 1916 by a designer working for a Bath shipbuilder who wished to accommodate wartime construction of Maine cargo schooners in a newly opened Georgia shipyard. Ole Hansen, a Webb Institute of Naval Architecture-trained designer and draftsman drew up a set of four-masted schooner plans for Percy & Small, shipbuilders, Bath, Maine, to dispatch to the Georgia Shipbuilding Company, Savannah, Georgia, along with a Bath-trained construction overseer. This Hansen schooner plan has survived in dim shards, photographically reduced, that have been carefully gathered and preserved by Captain W J Lewis Parker who kindly made them available for the purpose of this book. I am told that the schooners *Sally Wren* (1917), *Rosalie Hull* (1918), *Irene S. Wilkinson* (1918), and *Margaret Spencer* (1919), were laid down and completed at the Savannah shipyard per the Ole Hansen ship draught for 'Hull #1, Four Mast Schooner, 175' keel'. The Hansen plan depicts a vessel very close to the known measurements of the *Bertha L. Downs*. It represented, surely, the precipitate of forty years' experience in building this kind of vessel by the dozen at Bath, Maine. I felt that the authors owed the readers of this book the effort to reproduce every line of Ole Hansen's contemporary work as faithfully as possible. But it proved to be impossible. Those sheets had been photographed, enlarged and reduced so often that most of the lines were bent, or had grown, with lens distortion. The offsets, penned dimensions, and much of the captioning was shrunk or blotted to unreadability. But the vessel's overall drawings — the profile, the halfbreadths, the sections — and much of the structural detailing were usable if we went back to the Underwriter's Survey and heeded the as-built dimensions listed there.

The Hansen plan was redrawn and re-faired carefully, but to a much smaller scale for purposes of clear reproduction at book plate size. If you wish to build this schooner afresh at 200' +/– overall, you'd better plan to scale up to at least ¼in to 1ft which will yield a paper plan about 4ft long.

Then go to the loft floor for full size fairing of the offsets. The perspective drawings offered here are built upon the plane views by use of vanishing points and measured perspective technique.

These schoonermen made my graphics possible:

Captain W J Lewis Parker, USCG (Ret), a former crewman in the *T.K. Bentley*, saved from destruction and offered for this book the 1916 ship draught and specification sheets which underly my work.

Captain Douglas K Lee and Captain Linda Lee, builders, owners and operators of the windjammer schooner *Heritage*, of Rockland, Maine, for their willingness to share the active files of structural detail pertaining to Maine-built multi-masted schooners that they have compiled for an in-progress book of their own.

Mr James P Stevens, master shipbuilder, former crewman in the *Leona and Marion*, and now-retired president of Goudy & Stevens, Inc, shipbuilders, Boothbay, Maine, for his encouragement and oversight in my depiction of vessel structure that he knew well as a young man.

Captain Francis E Bowker, sailor, author, and inspirer of young people — for his oversight and commentary on the work that has been done. Alas, time ran out before I was able to fully pull the *Bertha*'s rig apart in perspective drawings. Biff Bowker would have enjoyed that.

The Maine Maritime Museum, Bath, Maine has been host or home to everyone involved with the *Bertha L. Downs* project. Nathan R Lipfert, Library Director, spent time with me reconstructing the Bath waterfront of 1908 and in locating the Hyde Windlass Co catalogues from which the *Bertha*'s deck equipment had been ordered.

There will be errors, but I hope not many. For these I take the rap.

SAM MANNING

Short Reading List

The literature of the schooners of the East Coast of North America is fairly extensive. The following works are relatively easily available for study in libraries.

WILLIAM A BAKER, *A Maritime History of Bath, Maine* (2 vols.), Bath 1973. A major work of historical research, this book contains a vast amount of information about the big schooners and their background.

FRANCES E BOWKER, *Hull Down*, New Bedford, Mass 1963. Written by a professional schoonerman and later a master, this is a first class account of the life of the *Helen Barnet Gring*.

——, *Blue Water Coaster*, Camden, Maine 1972. A first class, first hand, account of years of sailing in the later schooners.

——, *Herbert L. Rawding*, Mystic, Conn 1986. A very professional biography of this four-master.

ROBERT H BURGESS, *Coasting Schooner, The Four Masted* Albert F. Paul, Newport News, Va 1978. A biography of the vessel, well informed and readable.

——, *Sea, Sails and Shipwreck, Career of the four-masted schooner* Purnell T White. Also recommended.

—— (ed), *Coasting Captain. Journals of Captain Leonard S. Tawes Relating His Career in Atlantic Coastwise Sailing Craft from 1868–1922*, The Mariner's Museum, Newport News, Virginia 1967. Captain Hawes was Master of the three-masted *City of Baltimore* for over twenty years. This is an important source dealing with the economics as well as the handling of the vessels.

JOHN F LEAVITT, *Wake of the Coasters*, The Maritime Historical Association, Mystic, Conn 1970. Gives a first class account of the smaller New England coasting schooners.

PAUL C MORRIS, *Four Masted Schooners of the East Coast*, Orleans, Mass 1975. A useful reference book for the careers of individual vessels, but not always completely accurate.

W J LEWIS PARKER, *The Great Coal Schooners of New England*, The Marine Historical Association, Mystic, Conn 1948. This is the master work on the subject. See also Parker's chapter in *The Last Century of Sail* in the series *Conway's History of the Ship*, London 1993.

EDWARD W SMITH JNR, *Workaday Schooners*, Camden, Maine 1975. A very useful compilation with excellent photographs.

GILES M S TODD, *The Last Sail Down East*, Barre, Mass 1965. Another useful reference book.

The Photographs

The *Gov. Ames*, the first five-masted schooner to be built on the Atlantic coast of North America, was launched at Waldoboro, Maine, in 1888. She had a drop keel or centreboard, like a gigantic sailing dinghy. In her early years she rounded Cape Horn from east to west and crossed both the Pacific and the Atlantic. She is shown here light, that is, without cargo, and almost becalmed, off New York about 1898. The photograph illustrates the gaff topsails particularly well. (*W J Lewis Parker Collection*)

The six-master *Wyoming* was launched in 1909 at Bath, Maine, from the site now occupied by the Maine Maritime Museum. She was the largest American wooden sailing vessel to be operated in commercial service. (*Maine Maritime Museum*)

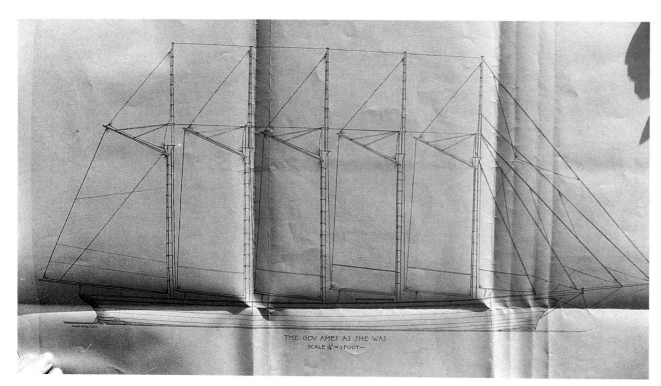

'The *Gov. Ames* As She Was' from a print of R B Forbes' drawing in W J Lewis Parker's collection.

Star Flyer, a successful barkentine-rigged cruise vessel of the 1990s, with a rig very similar to that advocated by R B Forbes more than a hundred years before. (*Fred Olsen Ltd*)

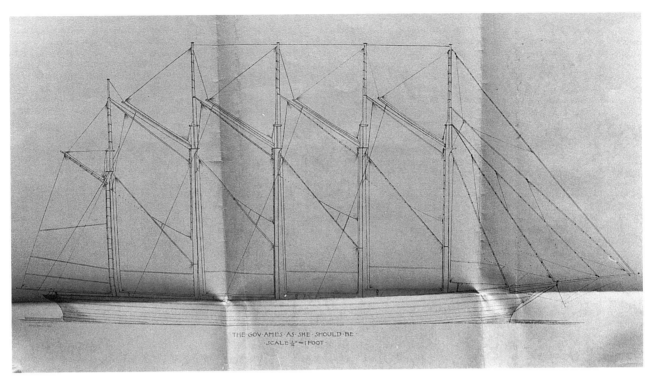

'The *Gov. Ames* As She Should Be', from a print of R B Forbes' drawing in W J Lewis Parker's collection.

'The medium size four-master . . . was among the most handsome, and certainly among the most efficient, wooden merchant sailing vessels ever to be constructed.' This is the *Robert M. McCurdy* built at Rockland, Maine, in 1903, and lost at sea in December, 1920. (*W J Lewis Parker Collection*)

The eight photographs which follow were taken of the Helen Barnet Gring in 1939 and 1940. They show many general features, rigging practices, etc, of a Maine built four-master, but it is to be remembered that the Gring was built eleven years after the Downs in a different part of Maine and under wartime conditions. For detail of the Downs, therefore, depend on the drawings.

Deck view on board *Helen Barnet Gring* on the port tack. Note the rail on turned stanchions which replaced the conventional bulwarks in many of the big schooners, but not in the *Bertha L. Downs*. (*Francis E Bowker*)

This photograph (the negative slightly damaged by seawater) shows the massive forestay, the tack of the forestaysail on its iron horse, the tack of the inner jib (standing jib in British schooner usage) the outer jib (boom jib) and the flying jib (same). (*Francis E Bowker*)

The main gaff topsail from the forecrosstrees. (*W A Funderburk thru' Francis E Bowker*)

Main gaff jaws and parrel, gaff topsail with the tack to windward of the gaff, deck view from high up in the starboard shrouds on the fore. (*W A Funderburk thru' Francis E Bowker*)

The foot of the mizzen with the boom jaws, the jigger and the after house, sunk into the deck, the yawl boat (a more or less standard piece of equipment in the big schooners) on the stern davits, the after hatches, the stern of a skiff carried on deck, the sheets of the main, laced to its boom. (*W A Funderburk thru' Francis E Bowker*)

'Boiling along in a fine fresh breeze', looking forward from the after end of the after house along the starboard side, the deckhouse forecastle occupies much of the width of the vessel. Note the rigging screws in place of deadeyes and lanyards. These were developed in Britain in the 1840s and gradually came into use during the rest of the century. (*W A Funderburk thru' Francis E Bowker*)

The vessel is on the port tack. The photograph shows the port side of the deck from aft. The washing is drying abaft the deckhouse forecastle. (*W A Funderburk thru' Francis E Bowker*)

The *Gring* is dwarfed by one of the great coal piers at Newport News, Virginia, which spelled the end for the schooners before the First World War. She has loaded a full cargo of coal for Bermuda in June 1940. The U.S. Flag painted on her port side is just visible. (*W A Funderburk thru' Francis E Bowker*)

The next three photographs were taken by G I Johnson of details of the rigging of the four-master **Herbert L. Rawding**, *built at Stockton Springs, Maine, in 1919.*

A shore rigger on the crosstrees of the foremast checks the rigging. The *Herbert L. Rawding* had been equipped with a new foremast. (*G I Johnson thru' Francis E Bowker*)

Detail of the bowsprit end, the jibboom and the martingale and rigging. (*G I Johnson thru' Francis E Bowker*)

Fitting the ironwork at the head of new foremast for the *Herbert L. Rawding* at Perth Amboy, New Jersey, in 1941. The shrouds have been made up and slid into place and the trestle trees and cross trees from the old mast adapted and fitted. This photograph gives an excellent impression of the massive size of the masts and fittings of a big four-master. (*G I Johnson thru' Francis E Bowker*)

The great five-master *Rebecca Palmer* leaving Fowey, Cornwall, under full sail and deep laden with china clay bound towards New York in July 1901. (*Fred Kitto thru' Basil Greenhill collection*)

A lumbering gang taking a break in the woods of Prince Edward Island, Canada. This was one of the sources of timber for building the schooners. (*B M 'Jack' Turner Collection, Public Archives of Prince Edward Island*)

The four-master *Jessie A. Bishop* nearly ready to launch at the Cobb Butler Company's yard at Rockland, Maine, in July 1908. The vessel in frame is the four-master *Lewiston* which was launched in September 1908, nine months after the launch of the *Bertha L. Downs* at Bath. (*W J Lewis Parker collection*)

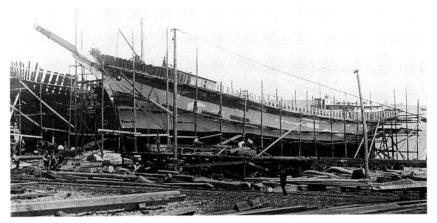

'The keelson was the main strength member in a big schooner.' This photograph shows the massive keelson of the *Rachel W. Stevens*, built by the New England Company in 1898. It comprises eight timbers of 16in squared pine scarfed together. The *Stevens* was lost off Cape Hatteras after twenty-six years of sailing. (*W J Lewis Parker collection*)

The *Bertha L. Downs* about to be launched on the morning of 16 January 1908. She is fully rigged with all sails bent. (*Maine Maritime Museum*)

This photograph of the six-master *Eleanor [A] Percy* on the slip at the Percy and Small [y]ard at Bath, Maine (now the site of the [M]aine Maritime Museum), in November [19]00 shows the lower masts stepped with [cr]oss-trees, the shrouds hanging loose, [m]ast hoops and bowsprit in position but [no]t the jibboom. (*Maine Maritime Museum*)

The *Bertha L. Downs* on arrival in Denmark with a cargo of oil cake in February 1917. (*Handels-og Sjøfartsmuseet på Kronborg*)

Atlas, ex *Bertha L. Downs*, discharging timber in Regents Canal Dock, London, in July 1927. She was by then an Åland Finnish vessel under the command of Captain Karl V Karlsson of Wårdö, Åland, but her second largest shareholder was Percy Appleby, shipbroker, of London. Astern of her lie the barks *Oaklands* and *Lalla Rookh*, both also owned in Åland. (*The late Captain Karl V Karlsson*)

Atlas at anchor in London River in the
1920s, deep laden with a big deck cargo.
(*The late Captain Karl V Karlsson*)

Captain Karl V Karlsson, seated second
from left, with his wife and eldest son and
Chief Mate Elis Mattsson, seated next to
him, and the crew of *Atlas* in Copenhagen
in 1930. (*The late Captain Karl V Karlsson*)

Atlas lying in Copenhagen in 1930. Five
members of the crew are showing off. (*The
late Captain Karl V Karlsson*)

Atlas deep laden on the port tack in The Sound off Copenhagen in the 1920s. (*The late Captain Karl V. Karlsson*)

Atlas, fore, main, and mizzen sails have been unbent from the gaffs which are being used as cargo booms for loading timber from barges in a Gulf of Bothnia roadstead. (*Ålands Sjöfartsmuseum*)

47

The Estonian-built and-owned four-masted schooner *Koit* sailing from Great Yarmouth, where she had discharged timber from Kemi in Finland, on 10 September 1938. (*David George*)

Atlas, a stern view. Registered at Pärnu, Estonia, she has been equipped with a single yard from which a flying squaresail could be set. Note the great length of the jiggerboom. (*National Maritime Museum of Sweden*)

Atlas, light, a bow view taken while she was registered at Pärnu. (*Dr Jürgen Meyer*)

The accommodation in a Maine-built four-master. The after house of the *James C. Hamlen*, built at Portland, Maine, in 1920, and in the 1930s, as the Estonian *Jaan*, a sister vessel to *Atlas*. (*W J Lewis Parker Collection*)

The *Martha* of Pärnu, ex *Clara Davis*, built at Mystic, Connecticut, in 1905 being dismantled in Copenhagen on 25 January 1938 after grounding off the Swedish coast when fully laden. She was subsequently towed over to Sweden where the hull was broken up. The photograph shows details of the deck structure of a contemporary of the *Downs*. (*Captain Søren Thirslund*)

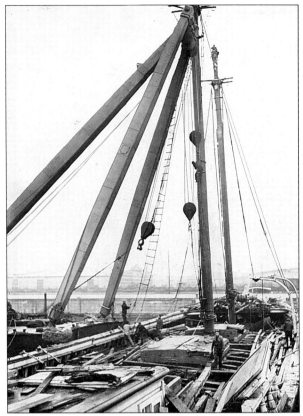

This retouched photograph shows a four-master with the look of a New England-built vessel: with doubled forestay; with no yard but with the crane from which the yard was slung still on the foremast; with a spike bowsprit in place of the bowsprit and jibboom and perhaps rigged with topmast staysails in place of her gaff topsails. The name *Atlas* has been touched in lower down on her bows, instead of on the topgallant rail of the foredeck, and part of her stemhead appears to be missing. She is loading timber from barges in a Gulf of Bothnia roadstead using the main and mizzen gaffs. This appears to be a photograph of an elderly vessel which has been quite extensively refitted. She is not the *Atlas*. It is possible that she is the *Martha* ex *Clara Davis*. (*Finnish Sawmill Owners Association*)

The *Gunn*, built at Victoria, British Columbia, Canada, in 1919, a sister vessel to *Atlas* in the Baltic trade, in Millwall Docks, London when she was owned in the Åland Islands and registered at Mariehamn. Note the raised poop and forecastle deck, typical of West Coast-built vessels. (*The late Captain F C Poyser*)

Yxpila, a Finnish-built four-master in the style of a West Coast of North America vessel, which sailed in the Baltic trade even at the height of the War in 1942 and 1943. (*Captain Søren Thirslund*)

A four-master which appears to have
outlived all others afloat was the *Annie C.
Ross* built at Bath, Maine, in 1917. She
survived the depression after the First
World War to become a successful vessel i
the lumber trade in the 1920s and 1930s.
She was laid up at New York in 1940 and
never went to sea again, but she was not
broken up until 1955. She is here shown
with the French liner *Normandie* in 1935.
(*Handels-og Sjøfartsmuseet på Kronborg*)

The Drawings

A General arrangement

A1   PROFILE (scale 1/16 inch = 1 foot)

A1

A General arrangement

A2 LINES PLANS

The *Bertha L. Downs* of 1908 was built from offsets or measurements taken from a wooden halfmodel and by established rules of thumb. Offsets from the model were drafted full size on the loft floor from which patterns for the vessel's frame pieces were picked up directly. Eight years later, wartime production of Maine-type schooners elsewhere in the country caused the need for scaled paper plans to be drafted in shipyards that had never needed them. It is from one of these sets of wartime plans for a four-masted schooner closely approximating the *Bertha L. Downs* that the following study has been derived.

A2/1 *Sheer and profile plan (scale ¹⁄₁₆ inch = 1 foot)*

A2/2 *Half breadth plan (scale ¹⁄₁₆ inch = 1 foot)*

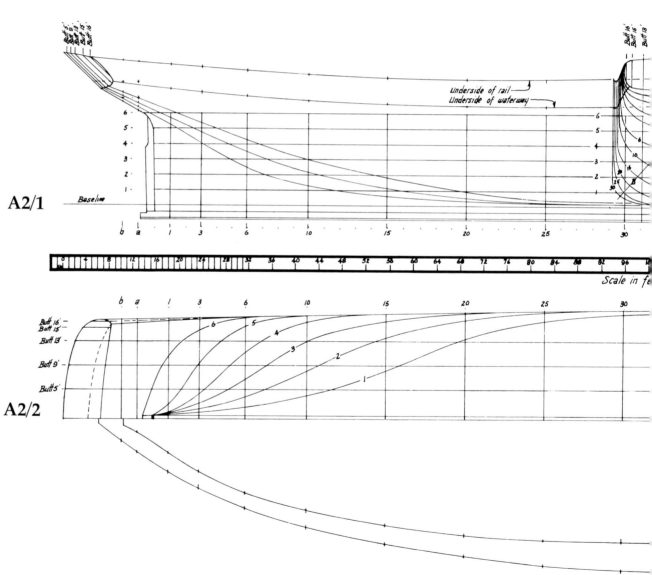

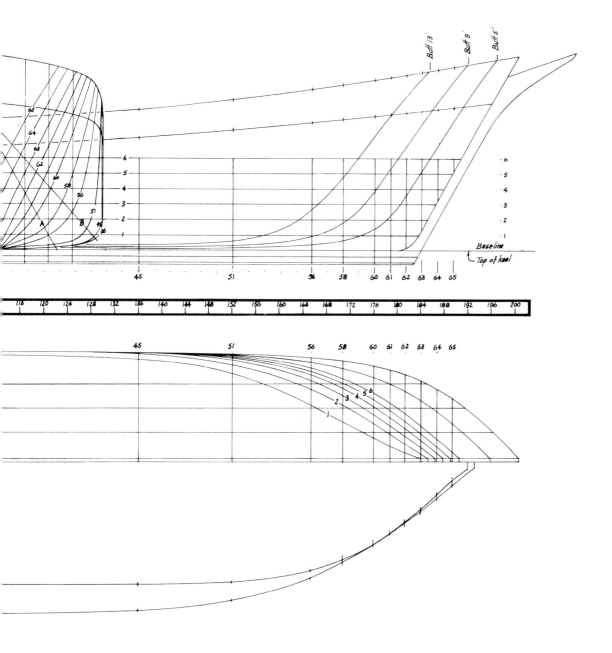

Butt 13'

Butt 9'

Butt 5'

6
5
4
3
2
1

6
5
4
3
2
1

Baseline
Top of keel

65 64 63 62 60 58 56 51 45

200 196 192 188 184 180 176 172 168 164 160 156 152 148 144 140 136 132 128 124 120 116

45   51   56 58 60 61 62 63 64 65

6
5
4
3
2
1

A2/3

Transom, stem and stern profiles

<table>
<tr><th></th><th>inside transom top</th><th>inside transom bottom</th><th>stern rabbet</th><th>stem rabbet</th></tr>
<tr><td colspan="5">Heights above baseline</td></tr>
<tr><td>u/s rail ℄</td><td>25·0</td><td>19·0</td><td></td><td></td></tr>
<tr><td>Butt. 5'</td><td>24·11</td><td>19·2</td><td></td><td></td></tr>
<tr><td>Butt. 9'</td><td>24·10</td><td>19·3</td><td></td><td></td></tr>
<tr><td>13'</td><td>24·9</td><td>19·5</td><td></td><td></td></tr>
<tr><td>15'</td><td>24·6</td><td>19·9</td><td></td><td></td></tr>
<tr><td>16'</td><td>24·0</td><td>21·0</td><td></td><td></td></tr>
<tr><td colspan="5">Distance aft of Sta ⓪ and forward of Sta ㉒</td></tr>
<tr><td>u/s rail</td><td></td><td></td><td></td><td>19·3</td></tr>
<tr><td>WL6</td><td></td><td></td><td>4·11</td><td>9·1</td></tr>
<tr><td>5</td><td></td><td></td><td>2·11</td><td>7·10</td></tr>
<tr><td>4</td><td></td><td></td><td>2·10</td><td>6·5</td></tr>
<tr><td>3</td><td></td><td></td><td>2·9</td><td>5·1</td></tr>
<tr><td>2</td><td></td><td></td><td>2·8</td><td>3·7</td></tr>
<tr><td>1</td><td></td><td></td><td>2·7</td><td>2·4</td></tr>
<tr><td>baseline</td><td></td><td></td><td>2·6</td><td>0·0·0</td></tr>
</table>

Waterlines are spaced 2'-6" except where indicated otherwise.
Stations are spaced 2'-8".
Offsets are measured to the nearest even inch.
Lines are drawn to the inside of the planking.

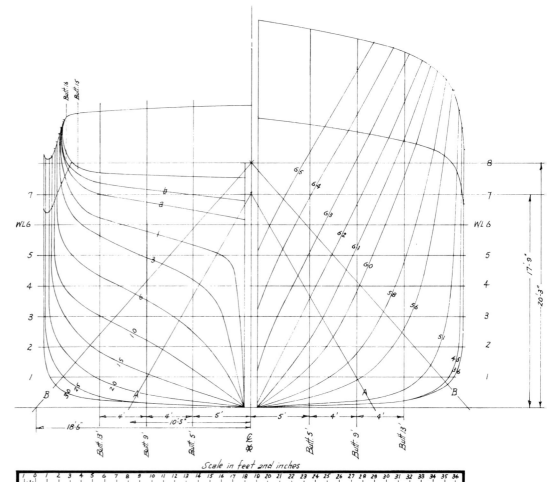

Scale in feet and inches

	Station #	Transom	b	a	1	3	6	10	15	20	25	30	36 ℄	45	51	56
Heights above baseline	Underside of rail	25·0	23·9	23·7	23·2	22·9	22·1	21·7	20·11	20·9	20·9	21·0	21·7	23·1	24·8	26·5
	u/s waterway	20·3	20·1	19·9	19·2	18·8	17·11	17·1	16·8	16·4	16·3	16·5	17·0	18·5	19·9	20·11
	Butt. 5'		17·6	16·3	13·5	10·6	6·2	3·1	1·5	0·6	0·3	0·2	0·2	0·3	0·5	0·11
	Butt. 9'		18·0	17·0	14·7	12·4	8·9	5·6	2·10	1·1	0·5	0·4	0·4	0·4	0·8	2·3
	Butt. 13'		18·7	17·8	15·8	14·2	10·9	7·6	4·7	2·3	0·11	0·8	0·8	0·8	1·6	6·7
	Rabbet		17·0	15·6	0·0·0	0·0·0	0·0·0	0·0·0	0·0·0	0·0·0	0·0·0	0·0·0	0·0·0	0·0·0	0·0·0	
Halfbreadths from ℄	u/s of rail	16·0	16·1	16·2	16·5	16·6	16·9	17·0	17·3	17·6	17·9	17·11	18·0	17·10	17·9	17·1
	waterway	15·7	15·8	15·10	16·1	16·5	16·9	17·0	17·3	17·6	17·9	17·11	18·0	17·10	17·6	16·5
	WL 1			0·8	1·1	1·11	3·11	8·0	13·3	16·0	17·4	17·4	16·10	14·7	9·5	
	WL 2			0·9	1·9	3·8	8·0	13·6	16·3	17·5	17·11	18·0	17·10	15·11	11·11	
	WL 3			1·0	2·6	6·7	12·11	16·0	17·4	17·9	17·11	18·0	17·10	16·8	13·6	
	WL 4			1·4	4·2	11·1	15·6	17·1	17·6	17·9	17·11	18·0	17·10	17·0	14·5	
	WL 5			2·6	9·3	15·4	17·0	17·3	17·6	17·9	17·11	18·0	17·10	17·2	15·0	
	WL 6			10·8	14·6	16·8	17·0	17·3	17·6	17·9	17·11	18·0	17·10	17·5	15·5	
Diagonals	Diag. A			2·3	5·9	8·8	12·1	14·11	17·4	19·0	20·1	20·0	20·3	20·3	19·9	17·10
	Diag. B		3·9	5·6	8·10	11·4	14·8	17·10	20·6	22·6	23·11	24·11	24·11	24·7	22·8	19·0

A3   LINES EXPANSION (no scale)

A3/1   Lines expansion showing measurement stations

1   Expansion of the hull lines on the drawing board by use of vanishing points and measured perspective. (This is a useful viewpoint of the lines matrix from which to examine the structure of the hull in drawings to follow.)

2   These numbered measurement stations relate to the numbered measurement stations in the sheer plan, the body plan and the half breadth plan (A2 above)

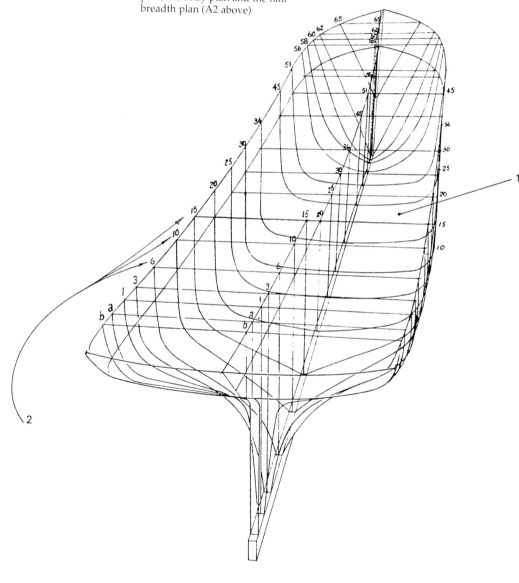

A3/1

	61	62	63	64	65	Stem rabbet
·0	28·5·	28·9	29·4·	29·10·	30·2·	32·0·
10	22·2	22·6·	22·10	22·11·	23·4·	24·6
5·	5·8·	9·1·	12·11·	17·6·	21·3·	
9·	13·5·	16·9·	20·8·	24·8·	28·0·	
·0	22·2·	25·6	28·4·	—		
·0	0·0·0	0·5·	3·1·	8·2·	13·0·	
9·	15·2·	14·5	13·5·	12·0·	10·5·	0·7·
⦁·	12·11·	11·8·	10·0·	8·4·	6·2·	0·7·
··	2·9·	1·7·	—	—	—	
··	4·7·	2·11·	1·2·	—	—	
··	6·1·	4·4·	2·3·	—	—	
··	7·5·	5·6·	3·6·	1·3·	—	
··	8·7·	6·8·	4·9·	2·5·	—	
··	9·9·	8·1·	6·1·	3·8·	1·7·	
··	11·11·	10·0·	7·11·	5·4·	3·0·	
··	11·11·	10·1·	8·3·	6·0·	4·0·	

59

A General arrangement

A3/2 *Overall view based on lines expansion*
1   Measurement stations appearing in
     the sectional views

A4   UPPER DECK PLAN (scale ¹⁄₁₆ inch
      = 1 foot)
A4/1 *Upper deck plan, poop and forecastle
      deck*
A4/2 *Forecastle deck*

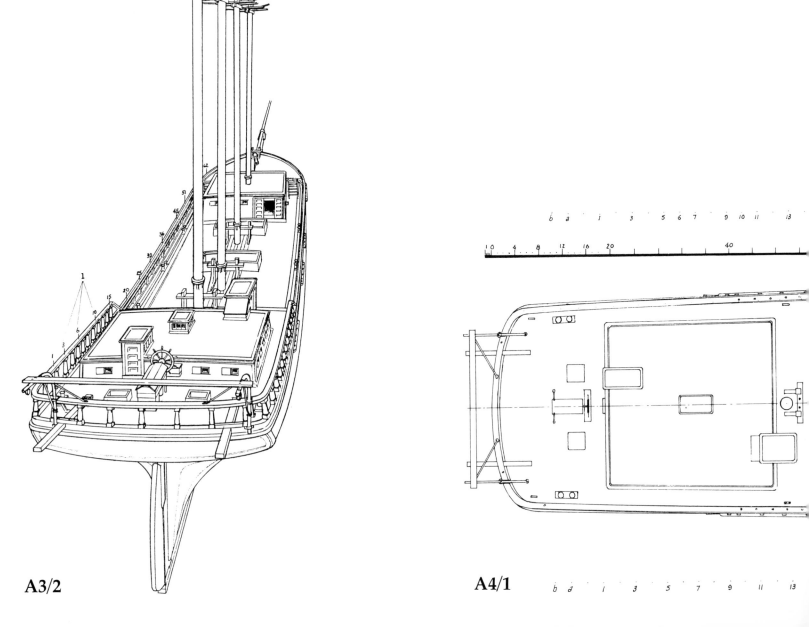

A3/2

A4/1

51 53 55 56 58 60 61 62 63 64 65

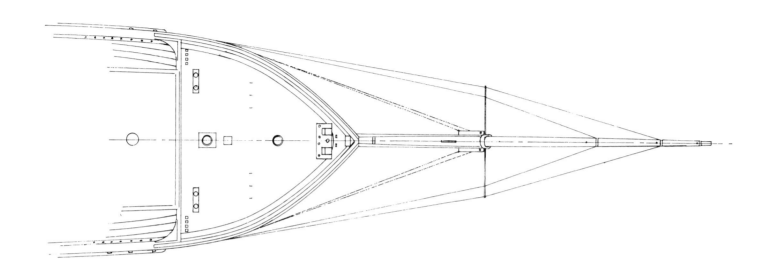

19 20 21 23 25 27 29 30 31 33 35 36 37 39 41 43 45 47 49 51 53 55 56 58 60 61 62 63 64 65

80 100 120 140 160 180 200

Scale in feet

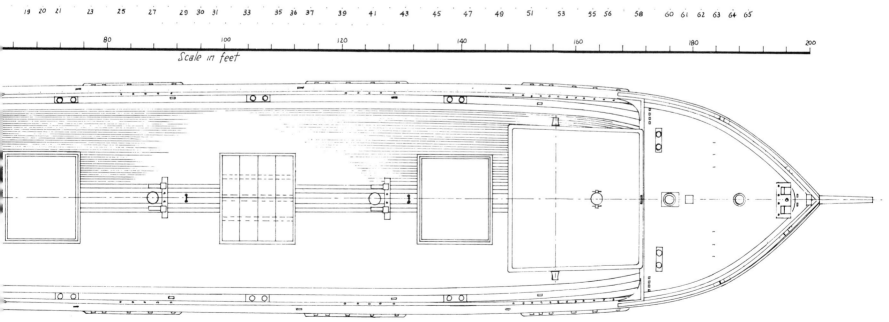

51 53 55 57 59 61 63 65

B Hull structure

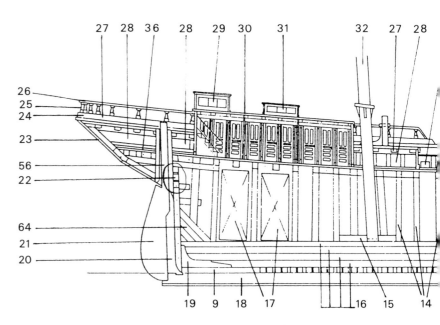

B1/1

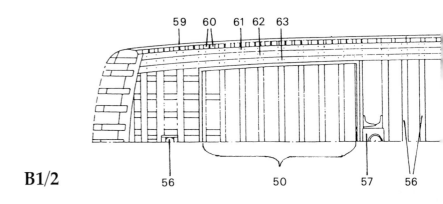

B1/2

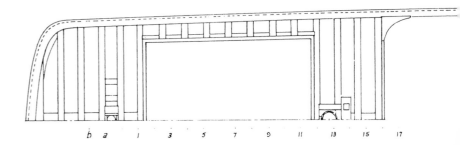

B1/3

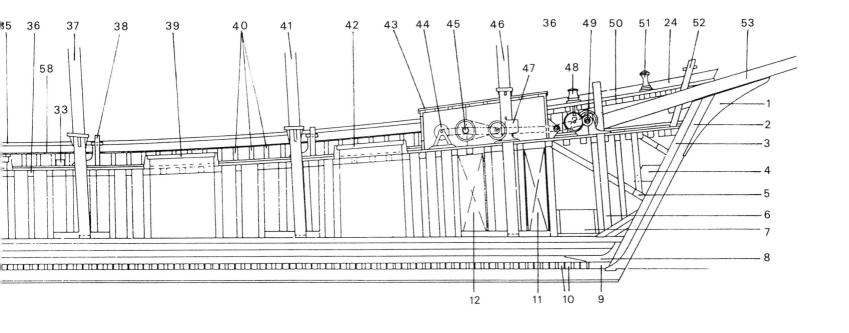

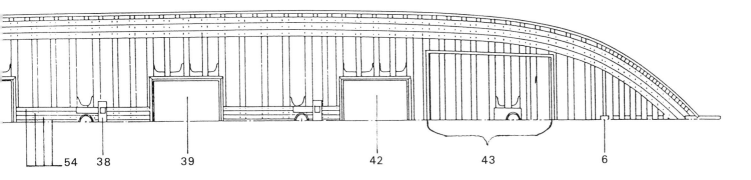

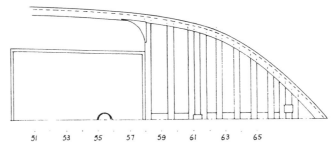

B1/4

B Hull structure

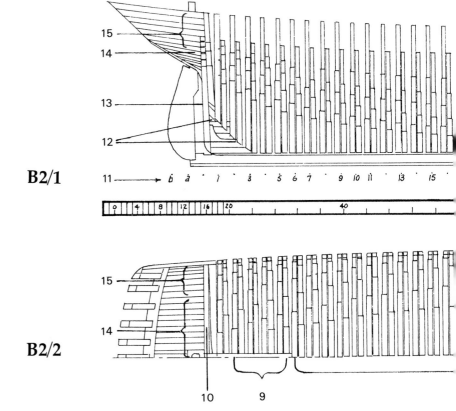

B2/1

B2/2

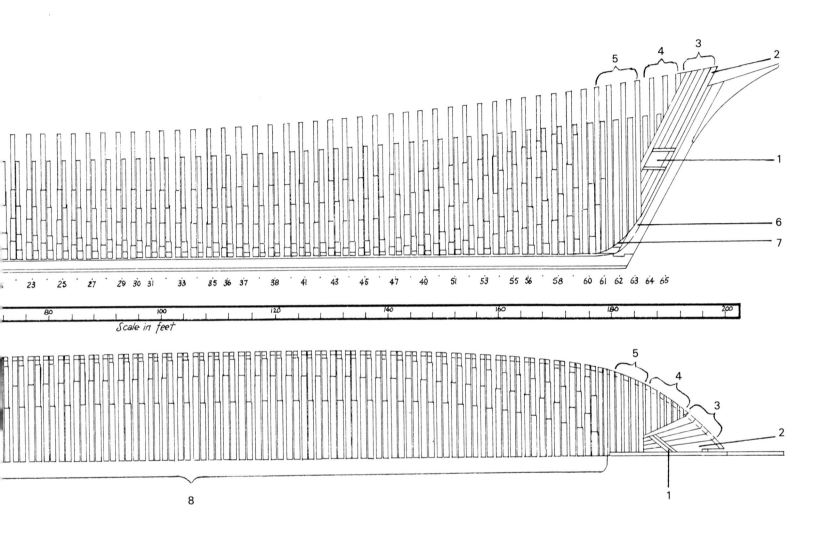

23　25　27　29 30 31　33　35 36 37　38　41　43　45　47　49　51　53　55 56　58　60 61 62 63 64 65

80　　　　100　　　　120　　　　140　　　　160　　　　180　　　　200

Scale in feet

8

B Hull structure

B3   INTERNAL CONSTRUCTION
      (no scale)

B3/1   *Disposition of timbers at station No 1*
       (looking forward)
1   Main deck rail (and poop deck
       coverboard)
2   Main deck planking
3   Main deck beams
4   Lodging knees
5   Mast partner (spanker)
6   Chock
7   Stanchion (hold)
8   Mast step (spanker)
9   Fresh water tank
10   Stanchion (hold)
11   Aft end of assistant keelson
12   Diagonal deadwood
13   1st frame futtock
14   3rd frame futtock
15   Bilge ceiling
16   5th frame futtock
17   Lock strake
18   Waterway timber
19   Planksheer
20   Top timber
21   Corner post, after deckhouse
22   Sills

B3/2   *Disposition of timbers at station No 1*
       (looking forward)
1   Spanker mast
2   Mast table
3   Fife rail
4   Coach house
5   Water table
6   Poop deck margin board
7   Poop deck planking
8   Hanging knee
9   Deck planking
10   Grub
11   Poop deck beam
12   Sill
13   Main deck beam
14   Hold stanchion
15   Bilge ceiling
16   Cabin/lazarette bulkhead
17   Poop deck clamp
18   Poop coverboard (and main rail)
19   Chock rail
20   Rail stanchion
21   Fly rail
22   House-top planking
23   After companionway
24   Fairlead rods
25   Skylight
26   Binnacle
27   Storm shutter
28   Clear sash

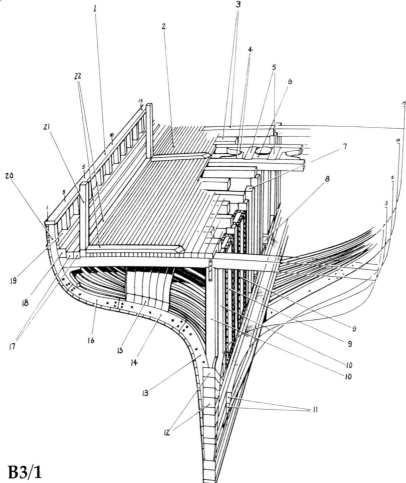

B3/1

B3/3   Disposition of timbers at station No 3
        (looking aft)
1   Waterway timber
2   Lock strakes
3   Deck plank
4   Long pup beam
5   Short pup beam
6   Deck beam
7   Rudder stock
8   Main rail/coverboard
9   Blocking
10   Stern timber
11   Stern fashion timber
12   Stern apron
13   Blocking
14   Counter timber (logged solid)
15   Transom
16   Fashion timber
17   Hull planking
18   Half frame (first futtock)
19   Ceiling
20   Hanging knee
21   Plank sheer

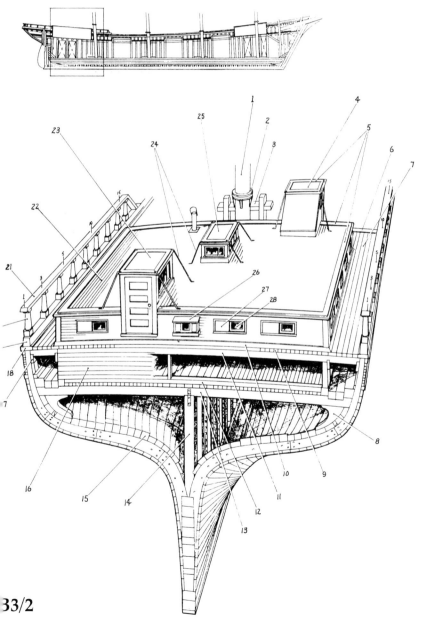

B3/2

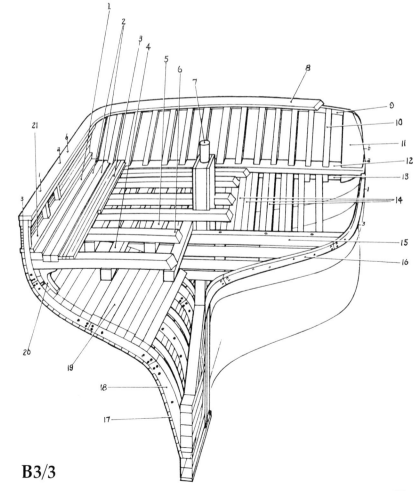

B3/3

B Hull structure

B3/4 *Disposition of timbers at station No 3*
(looking aft)

1	Poop deck planking	17	Hook
2	Main deck planking	18	Diagonal deadwood
3	Lazarette hatch carlin	19	Hull planking
4	Poop deck beam	20	Rudder blade
5	Turned stanchions	21	Rider keelson
6	Fly rail	22	Keelson (3 tiers)
7	Chock	23	Deadwood
8	Coverboard	24	Keel
9	Stern timber	25	Shoe
10	Stern apron	26	Pup beam
11	Counter timbers	27	Air strake
12	Fashion timber	28	Clamp
13	Transom	29	Poop deck short beam
14	Transom knee	30	Corner post, after cabin
15	Air strake	31	Grub
16	Hook	32	Sill

B3/5 *Disposition of timbers at station No 40*
(looking forward)

1	Main mast	23	Bilge ceiling
2	Mast table	24	Hanging knee
3	Fife rail	25	Air strake
4	Fife rail knee	26	Clamp timbers
5	Cargo hatch coaming	27	Sheer plank
6	Lodging knee – hatch	28	Planksheer
7	Main deck short beam	29	Bulwark plank
8	Hatch beam	30	Pin rail
9	Mast partner lodging knee	31	Main rail
10	Bilge extension ceiling	32	Chock rail
11	Floor ceiling	33	Thick centerline planking
12	Mast step timber	34	Mast wedges
13	Frame chock		
14	Short floor		
15	Long floor		
16	Rider keelson		
17	Assistant keelsons		
18	Keelsons		
19	1st garboard		
20	2nd garboard		
21	3rd garboard		
22	Limber board		

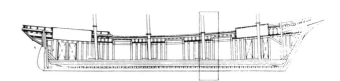

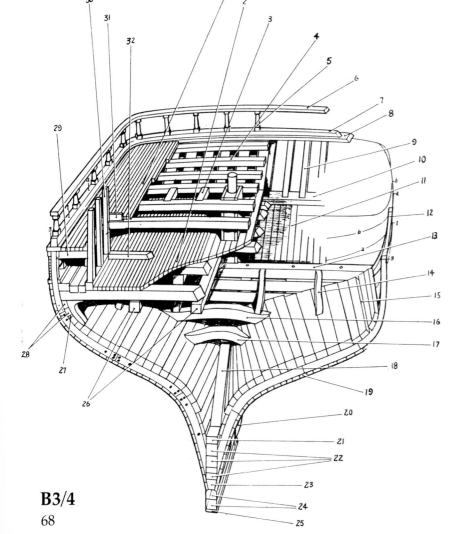

B3/4

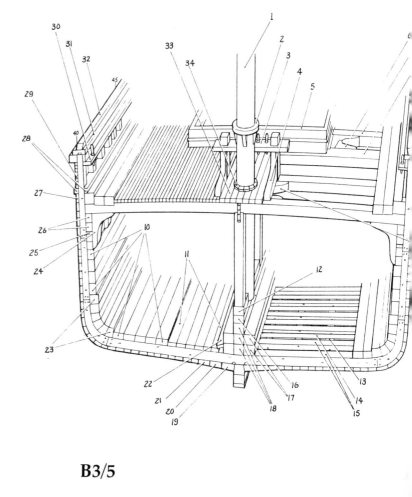

B3/5

'On the after part of the forward house, a baffle held rain water and directed it to a scupper on either side. A canvas hose led down to barrels on either side to collect the water. In heavy downpours the whole crew would gather to collect the water, fill the tanks, and try to save enough to wash clothes. This was the time for ''bucket baths''.' (*Capt. Biff Bowker, private correspondence*)

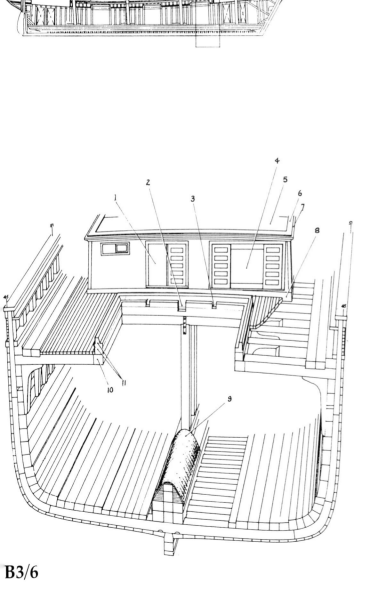

B3/6

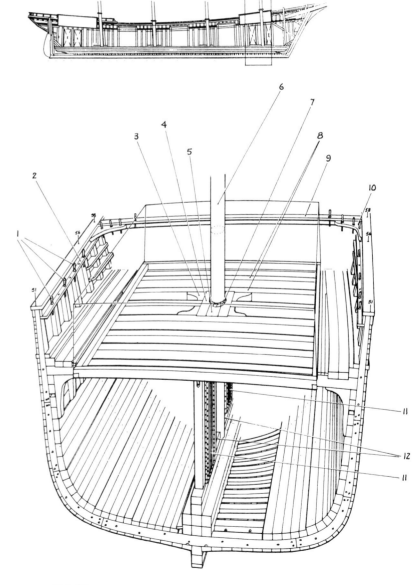

B3/7

B Hull structure

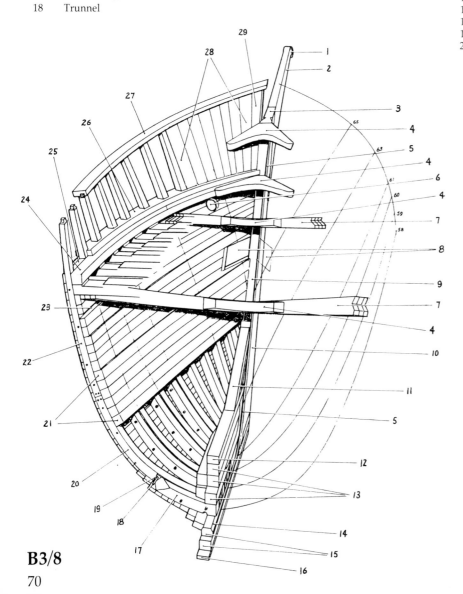

B3/8

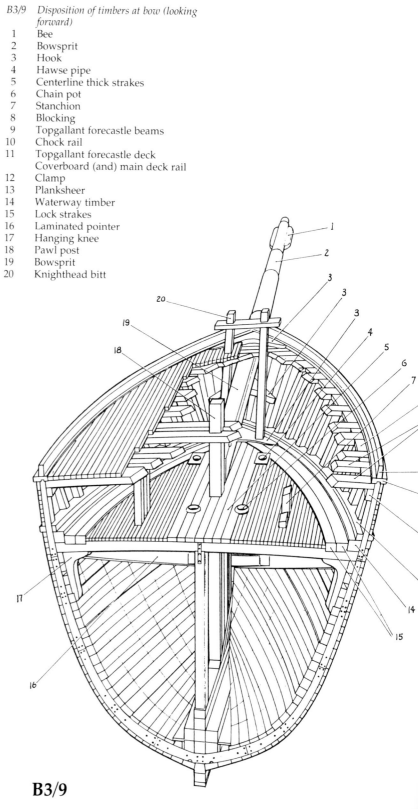

B3/9

70

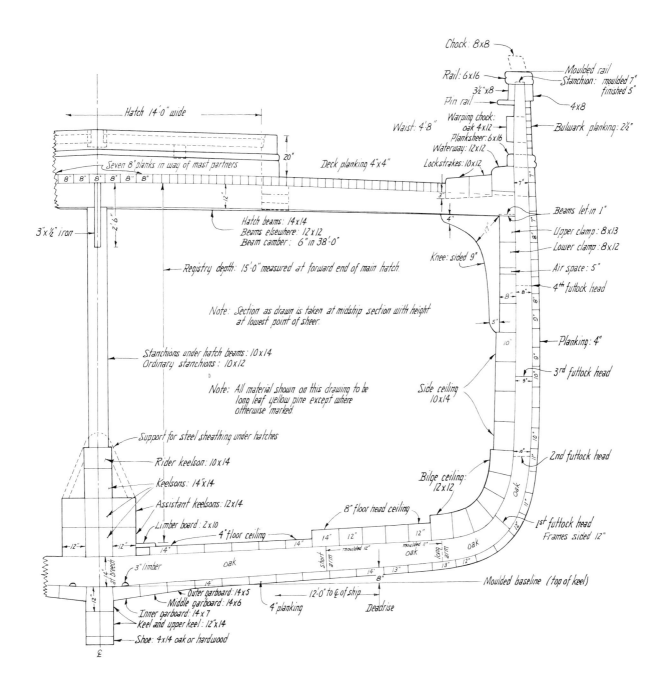

Chock: 8x8

Moulded rail

Rail: 6x16

Stanchion: moulded 7"
finished 5"

3½"x8

Pin rail

4x8

Warping chock:
oak 4x12

Waist: 4'8"

Bulwark planking: 2½"

Planksheer: 6x16

Waterway: 12x12

Lockstrakes: 10x12

Deck planking 4"x4"

Hatch 14'-0" wide

20"

Seven 8" planks in way of mast partners

8" 8" 8" 8" 8" 8" 8"

Beams let in 1"

Upper clamp: 8x13

Lower clamp: 8x12

Air space: 5"

4th futtock head

Hatch beams: 14x14
Beams elsewhere: 12x12
Beam camber: 6" in 38'-0"

Knee: sided 9"

3"x½" iron

2'-6"

Registry depth: 15'-0" measured at forward end of main hatch.

Note: Section as drawn is taken at midship section with height
at lowest point of sheer.

Planking: 4"

3rd futtock head

Stanchions under hatch beams: 10x14
Ordinary stanchions: 10x12

Note: All material shown on this drawing to be
long leaf yellow pine except where
otherwise marked.

Side ceiling
10x14

2nd futtock head

Support for steel sheathing under hatches

Rider keelson: 10x14

Bilge ceiling:
12x12

Keelsons: 14"x14

8" floor head ceiling

1st futtock head
Frames sided 12"

Assistant keelsons: 12x14

Limber board: 2x10

4" floor ceiling

14"   12"   12"

oak

short arm

moulded 12"   moulded   long arm   oak

14"

oak

12"

12"

3" timber

oak

14"

8"

Moulded baseline (top of keel)

Outer garboard: 14x5

12'-0" to ⊄ of ship

Middle garboard: 14x6

4" planking

Deadrise

Inner garboard: 14x7

Keel and upper keel: 12"x14

Shoe: 4x14 oak or hardwood

B4

B Hull structure

B5   STRUCTURE OF THE BOW PORTS
     (no scale)

B5/1   *Bow ports, seen from inboard*
 1   Hawse timber
 2   Knightheads
 3   Hull planking
 4   Trimmer
 5   Protective steel sheathing
 6   Stem
 7   Rabbet
 8   Through bolts, clenched or headed
 9   Bow port cover
10   Cleat
11   Eyes
12   Hooks
13   Strong back
14   Apron

B5/2   *Appearance of open bow ports in hulk of
       the* Alice B. Pendleton *in snapshots
       taken by Capt. Biff Bowker*

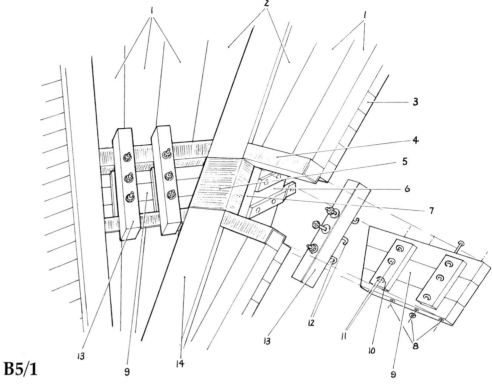

B5/1

B5/2

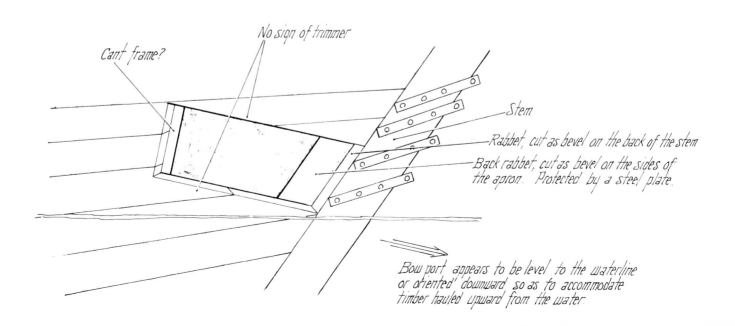

Cant frame?

No sign of trimmer

Stem

Rabbet, cut as bevel on the back of the stem

Back rabbet, cut as bevel on the sides of
the apron. Protected by a steel plate.

Bow port appears to be level to the waterline
or oriented downward so as to accommodate
timber hauled upward from the water.

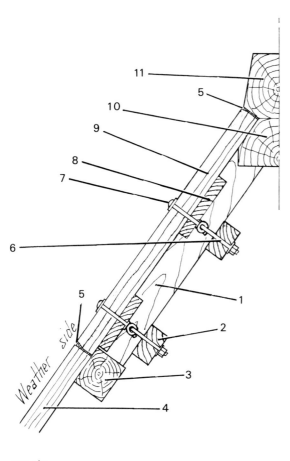

B5/3

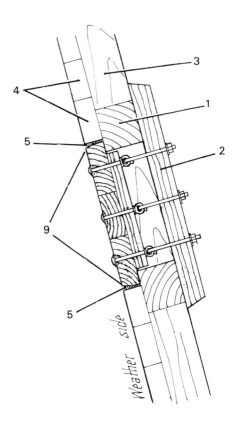

B5/4

B Hull structure

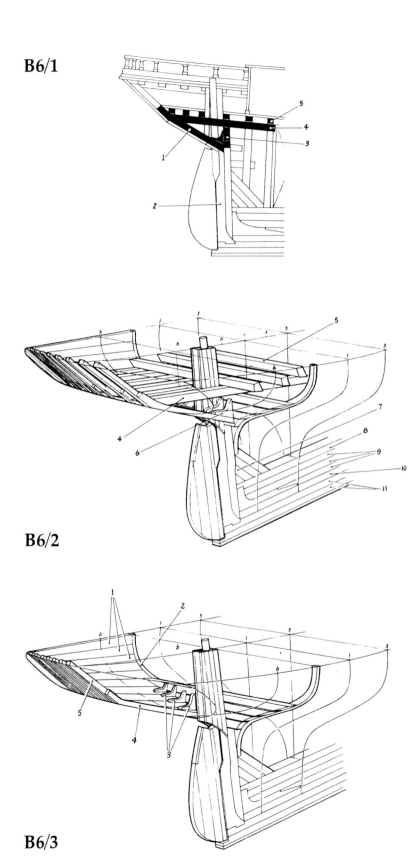

B6   STRUCTURE OF THE STERN
       (no scale)

B6/1   Profile of stern
B6/2   Disposition of timbers at stern
The counter is the whole stern structure abaft the stern post. In this class of vessel the counter is too broad and box-like to be supported successfully by a central horn timber and transverse frames that normally comprise the counter framework in a smaller, narrower, rounder-sterned vessel.

   Here the vessel's backbone terminates with the (inboard) structural transom. The counter is extended aft by means of pup beams rooted beneath deckbeams forward of the stern post and cantilevered over the structural transom. Pup beam, counter timber and the aft face of the transom are locked together in a rigid triangle which supports the weight of the structure above. Ten triangles under ten pup beams spread across the stern hold up the stern quarters in a way that a central horn timber could not.

1   Counter timber
2   Stern post
3   Transom
4   Pup beam
5   Deck beam
6   Counter timber knee
7   Diagonal deadwood
8   Rider keelson
9   Keelson (3 tiers)
10   Deadwood
11   Keel (2 tiers)

B6/3   Disposition of counter and stern timbers
This is a picture of the 'shell' of the schooner's counter minus the structure which holds it up. Those side counter timbers, or quarter blocking, are butted against the fashion timber. The bottom counter timbers butt against the transom and are kneed to it. The space between these counter timbers is logged solid with filler pieces to provide strong nailing for the bottom planking which crosses them obliquely. Ceiling, above the transom, will lie against the side counter timbers and be fastened to them.

1   Quarter blocking
2   Fashion timber
3   Counter timber knee
4   Counter timber
5   Stern timber

B6/1

B6/2

B6/3

The transom is set atop the inner sternpost and it
lays against the forward side of the sternpost. It is
made up of 12"×12" timbers blocked slightly apart
for ventilation and is drifted together with 1" dia.
drifts.

The fashion timber, sided 9", is bolted to the
forward side of the transom. The moulded shape
of this timber establishes the run of plank abaft
the transom to the stern, thereby forming the
shape of the counter.

The transom is basically an athwartship beam
in this type of hull structure. It is the foundation
for the counter. The planking of the stern at the
outboard face of the counter is the watertight
panel which today's sailors would term the
'transom'. It is called the 'stern' here.

Sternpost, inner sternpost, transom, rudder
trunk and the rudder itself are normally set up
atop the keel as a prefabricated unit during the
initial stages of construction.

1   Rudder stock
2   Rudder trunk (cut away)
3   Transom
4   Fashion timber
5   Stern planking
6   Stern timber
7   Counter timber
8   Transom
9   Rudder stock
10   Rudder blade
11   Stern post
12   Inner stern post
13   Stern knee
14   Keel
15   Shoe

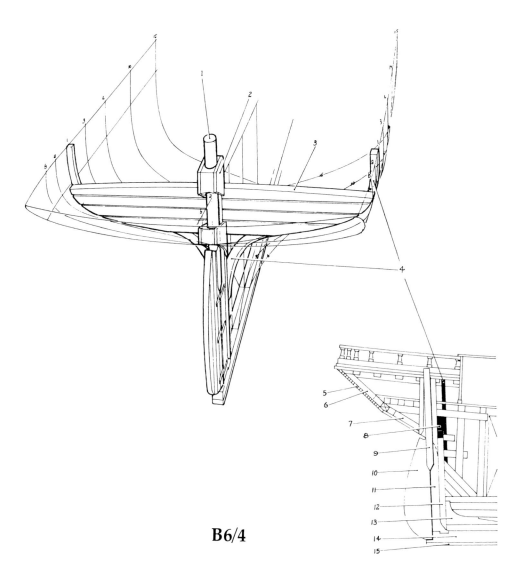

B6/4

C Deckhouses and hatches

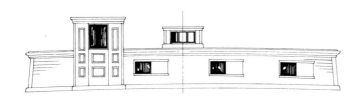

C1/1

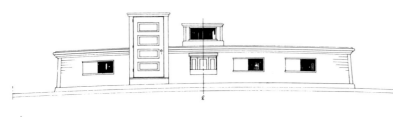

C1/2

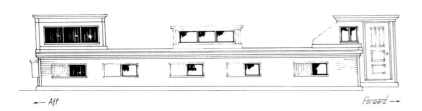

C1/3

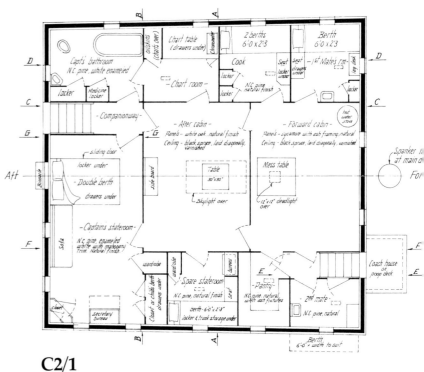

C2/1

C2/2

C2/3

C2/4

C2/5

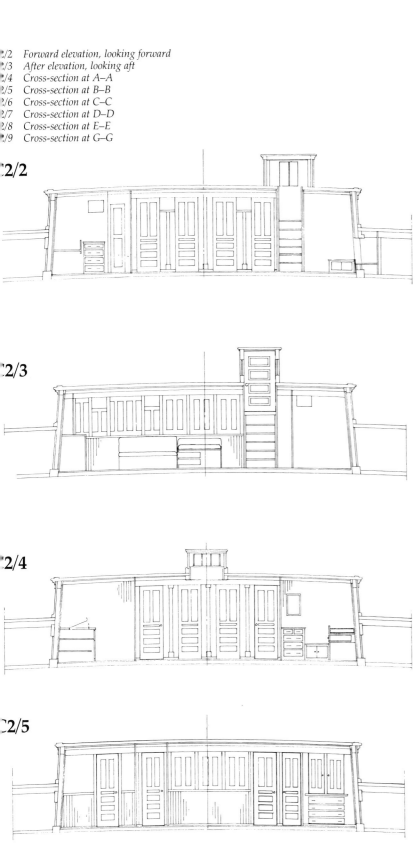

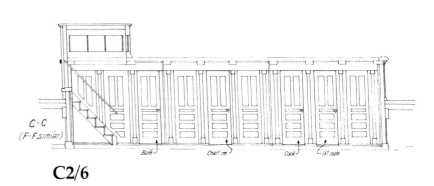

C2/6

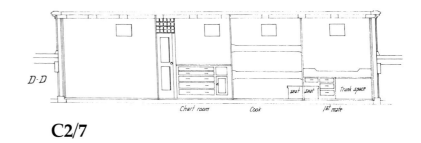

C2/7

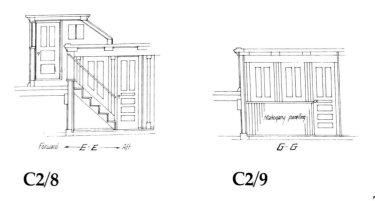

C2/8

C2/9

77

C Deckhouses and hatches

C3 AFTER ACCOMMODATION
(no scale)

C3/1 *Plan as sketched by Captain Karl V Karlsen*

C3/2 *Plan in perspective*
1 Coal furnace
2 Forward cabin (officers' mess)
3 Second mate's stateroom
4 (Bunk is beneath the side deck)
5 Pantry
6 Spare stateroom
7 After cabin (main salon)
8 Captain's stateroom
9 Captain's bathroom
10 Chart room
11 Cook's stateroom
12 First mate's stateroom

'This drawing reminds me of the (cabin) arrangement aboard the *Herbert L. Rawding*. She had steam radiators instead of the coal stove. One thing to remember: overhead in the captain's bathroom was a rectangular tank for fresh water to wash with. It may also have been used to flush the head. This bathroom was for the captain and guests only. Mates went forward for toilet and to obtain water for their sinks. Whenever there was heavy rain and the decks were dry, the decks would be rinsed, the scuppers plugged and all barrels and tanks would be filled with water either collected on deck or within barrels placed to collect rainwater from scuppers which drained the tops of the deckhouses.' (*Capt. Biff Bowker, commenting on this drawing*)

C3/3 *Projection at top of deckhouse*

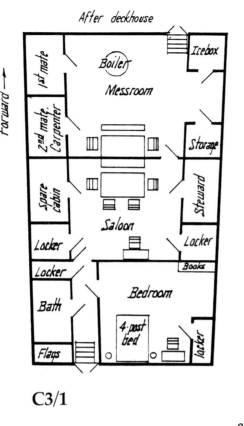

C3/1

C3/2

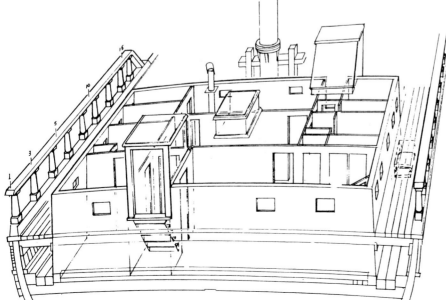

C3/3

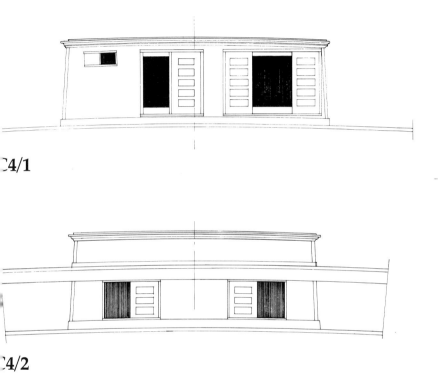

C4/1

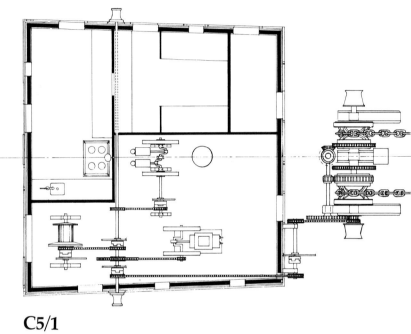

C5/1

C4/2

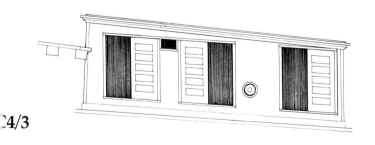

C4/3

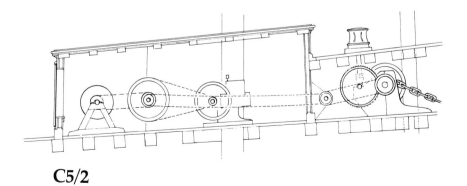

C5/2

C Deckhouses and hatches

C5/3 Machinery in the forward deckhouse
1. Gypsy head
2. Power transmission shaft
3. Bilge pump (port and starboard suction)
4. 12 hp gasoline hoister engine
5. Messenger chain: motor to power shaft
6. Clutch
7. Messenger chain: power shaft to windlass
8. Messenger chain: shaft to hoister
9. Hoister drum
10. 3″ limber holes
11. Freshwater tank
12. Hold stanchion
13. 3″ dia. bilge pump suction, starboard. (Similar suction pipe on port side)

C6   FORWARD ACCOMMODATION
         (no scale)

C6/1   Plan as sketched by Capt Karl V Karlsen

C6/2   Forecastle berths
1. Mess table (with transmission shaft under)
2. Forecastle with berthing for 4 men
3. Bosun's locker
4. Engine room
5. Galley
6. 'Pie hole'

'In a vessel the size of the *Bertha L. Downs*, there would usually be four berths in the forecastle and a table (probably folding) by the ''dog hole'' or ''pie hole''. Vessels I sailed in usually had the bosun's locker in the lazarette back aft where crews could not easily steal stuff to sell in port. ''Different ships different long splices'' was an old saying.' (*Capt. Biff Bowker, personal correspondence*)

C6/3   Galley
1. Galley
2. 'Pie hole'
3. Forecastle
4. Bosun's locker
5. Fore mast
6. Charlie noble
7. Shipmate cook stove
8. Power transmission shaft

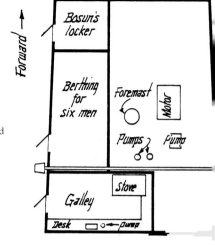

C6/1

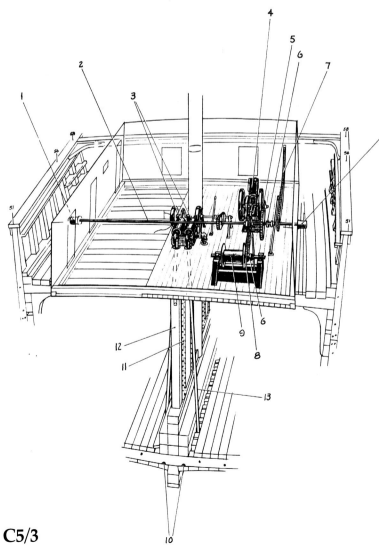

C5/3

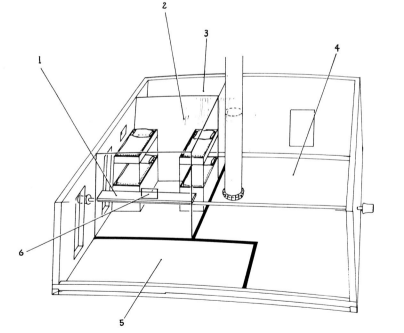

C6/2

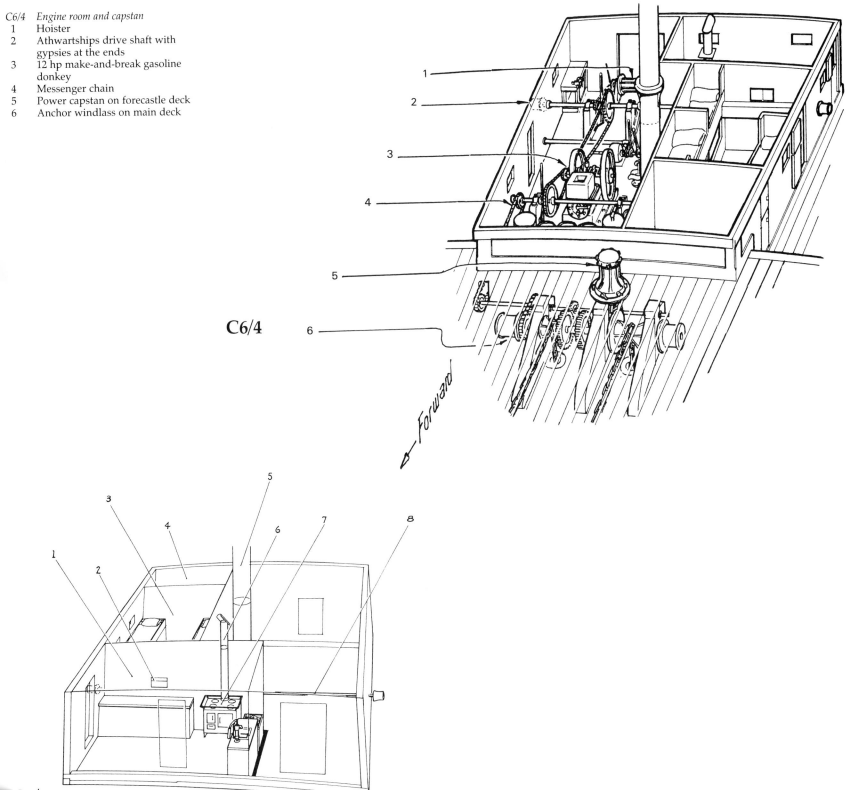

C6/4 *Engine room and capstan*
1   Hoister
2   Athwartships drive shaft with
     gypsies at the ends
3   12 hp make-and-break gasoline
     donkey
4   Messenger chain
5   Power capstan on forecastle deck
6   Anchor windlass on main deck

C6/4

Forward

C6/3

C Deckhouses and hatches

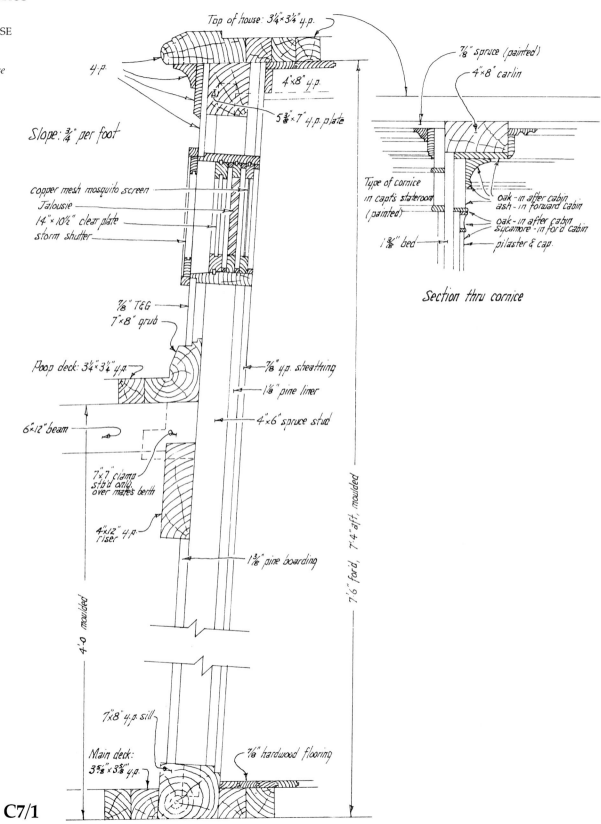

Top of house: 3¼"×3¼" y.p.

7/8" spruce (painted)

4"×8" carlin

4:p.

4"×8" y.p.

Slope: ¾" per foot

5⅜"×7" y.p. plate

Type of cornice
in capt's stateroom
(painted)

oak – in after cabin
ash – in forward cabin

copper mesh mosquito screen

oak – in after cabin
Sycamore – in for'd cabin

Jalousie

1⅜" bed

pilaster & cap.

14"×10½" clear plate

storm shutter

Section thru cornice

7/8" T&G
7"×8" grub

Poop deck: 3¼"×3¼" y.p.

7/8" y.p. sheathing

1⅛" pine liner

6"×12" beam

4"×6" spruce stud

7"×7" clamp
stb'd only,
over mate's berth

4"×12" y.p.
riser

1⅜" pine boarding

7'6" for'd, 7'4" aft, moulded

4'-0 moulded

7"×8" y.p. sill

Main deck:
3⅝"×3⅝" y.p.

7/8" hardwood flooring

C7/1

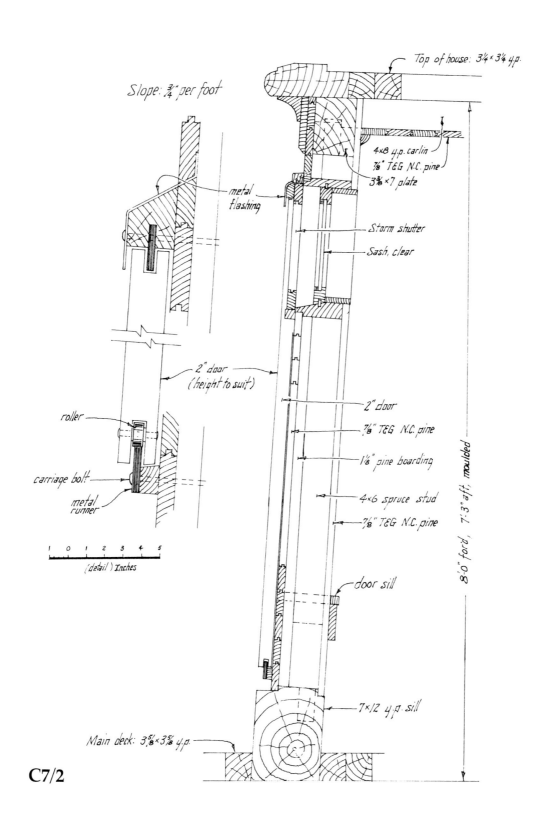

Slope: ¾" per foot

Top of house: 3¼ × 3¼ y.p.

4×8 y.p. carlin

⅞" T&G N.C. pine

3¾ × 7 plate

metal flashing

Storm shutter

Sash, clear

2" door
(height to suit)

2" door

⅞" T&G N.C. pine

1⅛" pine boarding

roller

4×6 spruce stud

⅞" T&G N.C. pine

carriage bolt

metal runner

door sill

8'-0 fo'd, 7'-3" aft, moulded

7×12 y.p. sill

| 1 0 1   2   3   4   5
(detail) Inches

Main deck: 3⅝ × 3⅝ y.p.

C7/2

83

C Deckhouses and hatches

C8   CARGO HATCH (no scale)

C8/1   Construction
1   Hatch beam
2   Hold stanchions or pillars
3   Header, aft lower piece
4   Hatch carling or trimmer
5   Fore and after, lower piece
6   Header, forward lower piece

C8/2   Details
1   Metal sheathing, interior face
2   Angle-bar edging
3   Snatch block staples, port and
     starboard
4   Hatch batten hanger bolts
5   Hatch strongback tiedown eyebolts
6   Header, aft upper piece
7   Iron strap facing atop the coaming
8   Lifting ringbolt
9   Hatch covers
10   Ridge beam
11   Fore and after
12   Iron strap facing atop the coaming

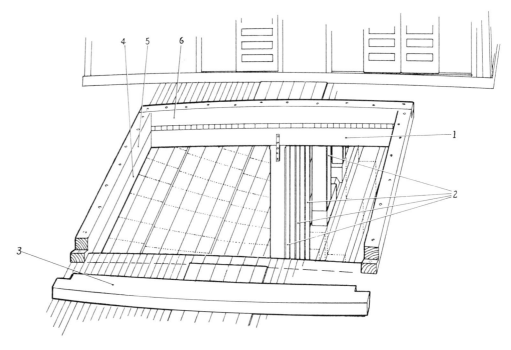

C8/1

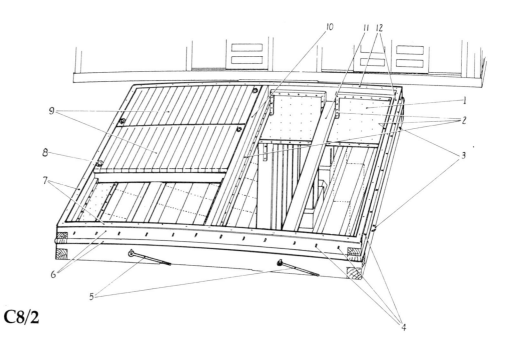

C8/2

1 Ridge beam
2 Fore and after
3 Hatch covers
4 Strong back
5 Hatch tarpaulins (3 layers in summer, 5 layers in winter)
6 Hatch battens: ½″ × 3″ iron flat bar pierced for hanger bolts which, with nuts outward, compress the canvas against the hatch coaming

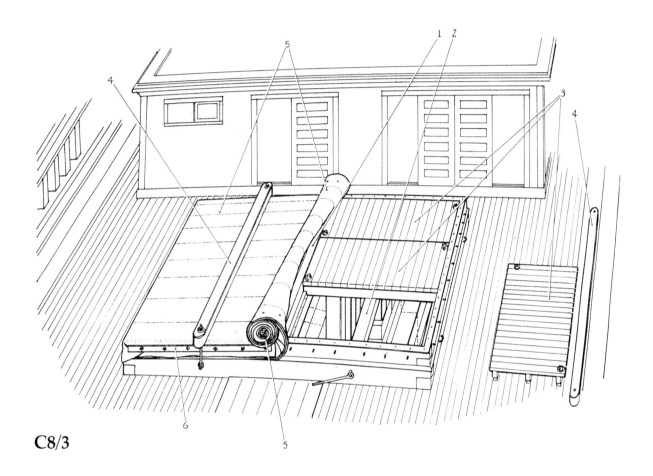

C8/3

D Fittings

D1   RUDDER STOCK AND RUDDER
         TRUNK (no scale)

D1/1   *Profile*
D1/2   *Rudder stock and blade*
D1/3   *Stern post fittings*
D1/4   *Rudder trunk*
D1/5   *Detail of rudder trunk*

The *rudder stock* is of white oak, 17" in diameter,
formed in one piece with the forward plank of the
rudder blade. Remainder of the blade is of hard
pine, 10" thick at bottom, and 14" at the tip.

   The *rudder trunk* is of hard pine with pieces
splined, luted and through-bolted or banded
together. The rudder trunk extends from exterior
of the hull planking to the weather surface of the
deck. It is made watertight with white pine shims
at both ends.

1   Rudder trunk must provide
     clearance for unshipping of the
     rudder for repairs
2   Rudder stock
3   Through bolts
4   Rudder blade
5   Pintle
6   Lock block
7   Stern post
8   Inner stern post
9   Gudgeon or brace
10   Hollowed and coppered
11   Rudder trunk
12   Side planking. (Other side removed)
13   Lock block
14   Stern post
15   Lock block. (To keep the rudder
     from lifting and unshipping
     accidentally)
16   Through bolted
17   (If banded)
18   Hole elongated to allow withdrawal
     of the rudder stock for repairs

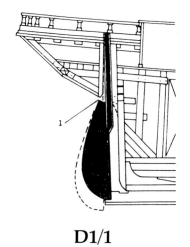

D1/1

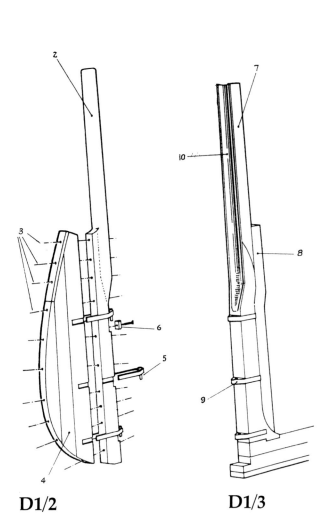

D1/2

D1/3

D1/4

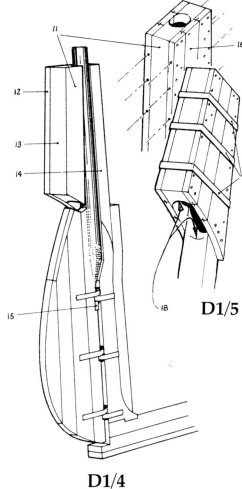

D1/5

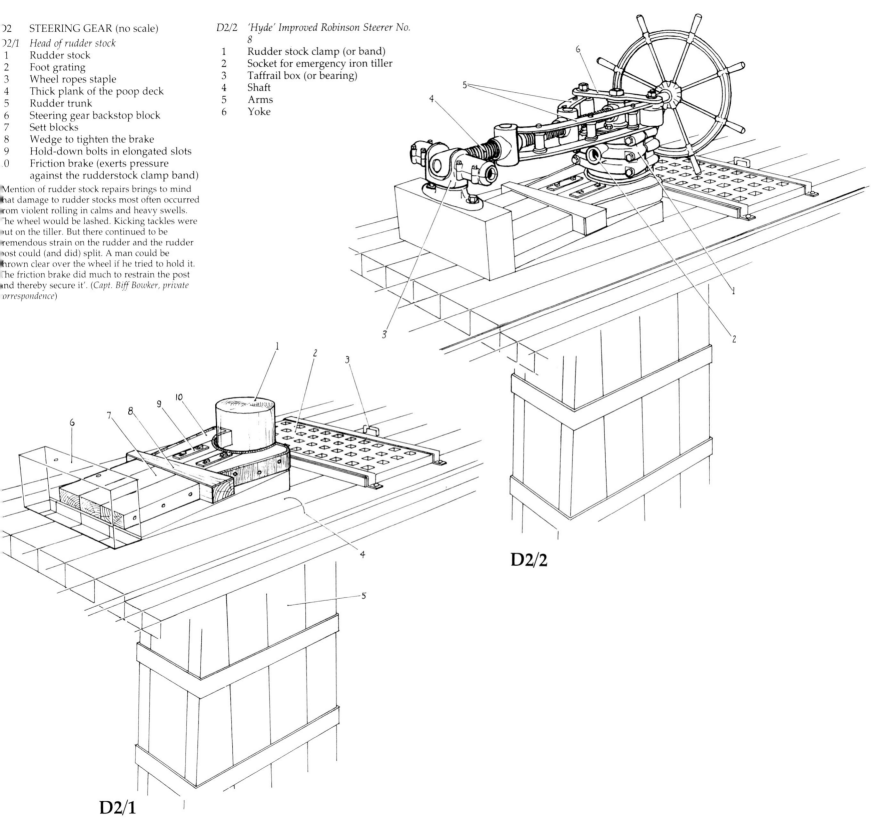

D2   STEERING GEAR (no scale)

D2/1   *Head of rudder stock*
1   Rudder stock
2   Foot grating
3   Wheel ropes staple
4   Thick plank of the poop deck
5   Rudder trunk
6   Steering gear backstop block
7   Sett blocks
8   Wedge to tighten the brake
9   Hold-down bolts in elongated slots
10   Friction brake (exerts pressure
       against the rudderstock clamp band)

Mention of rudder stock repairs brings to mind
that damage to rudder stocks most often occurred
from violent rolling in calms and heavy swells.
The wheel would be lashed. Kicking tackles were
put on the tiller. But there continued to be
tremendous strain on the rudder and the rudder
post could (and did) split. A man could be
thrown clear over the wheel if he tried to hold it.
The friction brake did much to restrain the post
and thereby secure it'. (*Capt. Biff Bowker, private
correspondence*)

D2/2   *'Hyde' Improved Robinson Steerer No.
8*
1   Rudder stock clamp (or band)
2   Socket for emergency iron tiller
3   Taffrail box (or bearing)
4   Shaft
5   Arms
6   Yoke

D2/2

D2/1

87

D Fittings

D2/3 Steering system with wheel box in place

1. Steering wheel
2. Staple for wheel ropes
3. Foot grating
4. Shoe of the friction brake
5. Wedge to tighten brake
6. Sett blocks
7. Rudder trunk
8. Rudder blade
9. Rudder stock
10. Stern post
11. Thick plank of the poop deck
12. Steering gear block
13. Wheel box

D3   BILGE PUMPS (no scale)

D3/1 Bilge pump, aft (manually operated)

1. Pump body
2. Plunger
3. Level socket
4. Lever or brake
5. Suction pipe housing
6. Starboard suction pump
7. Port suction pump
8. Suction pipe
9. Strainer
10. Spanker mast
11. Poop deck
12. Main deck lazarette space just forward of the after deck house
13. Limber holes

This is a plunger type suction pump of the Russell pattern made available by the Hyde Windlass Company of Bath, Maine under its own patent. The bent brake handle allowed the pump to be operated from either a standing-up or (with bend reversed) a bending-over position. These pumps drained sumps alongside the sister keelsons, port and starboard, just abaft the spanker mast.

The suction pipes, one on each side of the keelson assembly, were housed similarly to the suction pipes of the forward bilge pumps (drawing D3/2) in order to prevent them from being choked or damaged by bulk cargo pressing against them. The housing is not shown in this drawing.

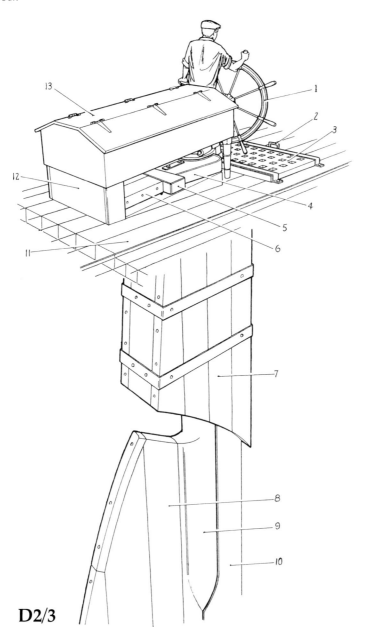

D2/3

D3/1

88

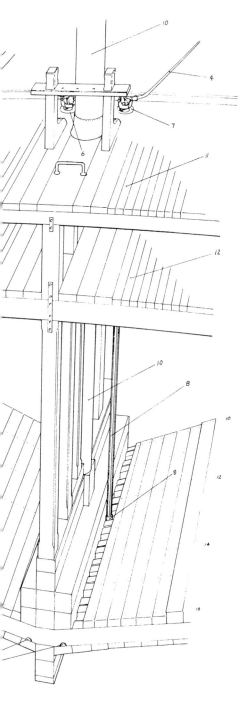

D3/2 *Forward bilge pump*
1. Fore mast
2. Bilge pump suction pipe (port and starboard bilges) connects to powered wrecking pump directly above in the hoister engine room
3. Suction pump housing (shown cut away on starboard side, bottom)
4. Fresh water tank is located atop the rider keelson in this bay
5. Lower end of the bilge pump suction pipe in sump between floor timbers

'I am certain there was a housing around the [pump suction] pipe because it had to come outside of the sister keelson and the strainers would reach down into the limbers on each side. The limber strake could be removed for cleaning if the hold was empty but not much could be done if the vessel began to leak with cargo in her. I seem to remember that the pump shaft could be lifted out and the strainer cleaned but that wouldn't help much if the limbers were clogged with coal or salt at sea.' (*Capt. Biff Bowker, private correspondence*)

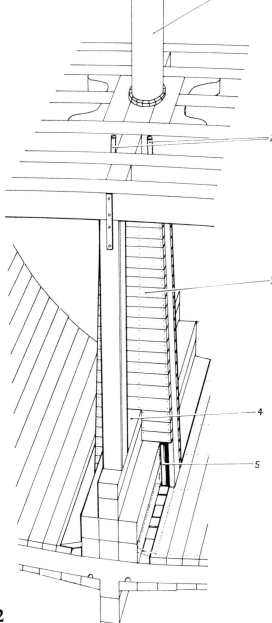

D3/2

D Fittings

D4 WINDLASS (no scale)

D4/1 Power train to windlass

1 Forward bulkhead of forward deckhouse
2 Gypsy head
3 Levelling block
4 Powered winch head
5 Pawl post
6 Main driving gear
7 Wildcat for 1¹⁄₁₆" chain
8 Compressor (controls the wildcat brake band)
9 Wildcat brake drum
10 Hawse pipe (inboard end)
11 Gypsy head
12 Messenger chain

13 Clutch
14 Hoister gypsy head
15 Power transmission shaft
16 Hoister motor: American Buffalo 5 hp make & break gasoline engine
17 Port bitt
18 Center bitt
19 Starboard bitt
20 Chain pot

'A messenger chain would lead from the engine, forward to the windlass. Gasoline and kerosene drums might be stowed under the forecastle head. These fuels were sometimes stowed in the engine room. That was a good place for fires to start.' (*Capt. Biff Bowker, private correspondence*)

D4/2 Forecastle deck arrangement

1 Knighthead bitt
2 Belaying pin
3 Jib sheet fairleads
4 Bow chock
5 Hand capstan
6 Pawl post
7 Brake drum compressor, starboard anchor chain wildcat
8 Access hatch to chain locker
9 Starboard anchor chain
10 Starboard anchor chain locker
11 Port chain locker
12 Port anchor chain
13 Margin plank, topgallant forecastle deck

14 Corner post, forward deck house
15 Chock rail
16 Brake drum compressor
17 Powered winch head

'This drawing needs some sort of platform for the man stowing chain. [Done – within limits of viewability – SFM] Only an idiot would stand in the locker because chain often slipped on the wildcat and a few links would fly out. This was usually due to twists in the chain if she had swung to the tide for a period of time. . . . The *Downs* was probably not large enough to have a ''head'' under the forecastle deck. A bucket in the engineroom would serve.' (*Capt. Biff Bowker commenting on an earlier draft of this drawing*).

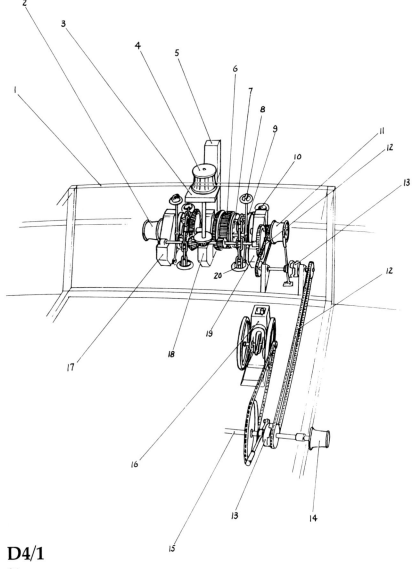

D4/1

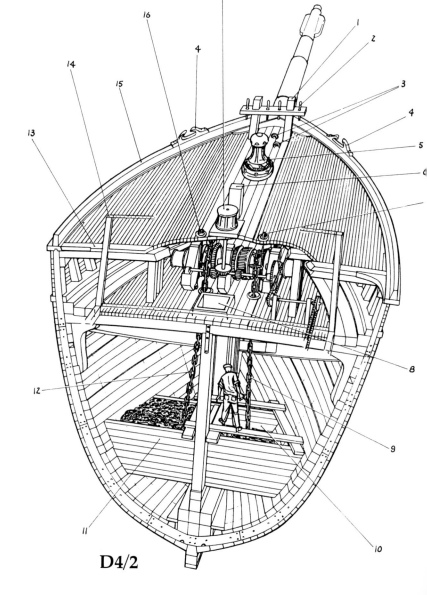

D4/2

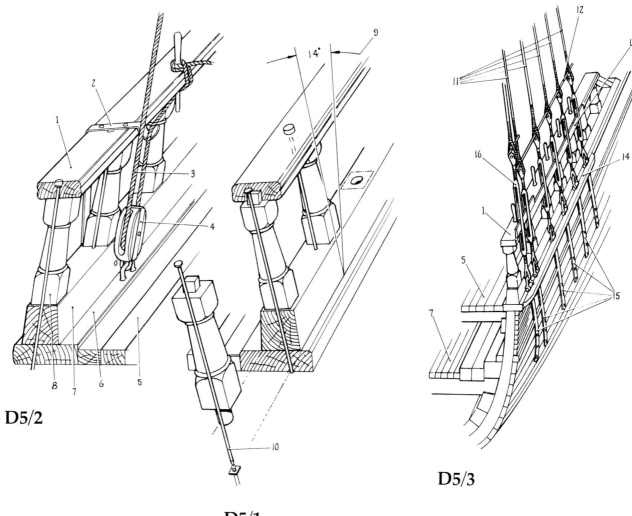

D5/2

D5/1

D5/3

D Fittings

D6 BULWARKS (no scale)
1 Bullseye fairleads for headsail sheets
2 Steps to the topgallant forecastle deck
3 Main deck at forward house
4 Halyard fairlead hook
5 Halyard fairlead block
6 'Waterway' area, extending from bow to stern
7 Deck beam
8 Hanging knee
9 Ceiling
10 Bulwark
11 Chain plates
12 Fore halyard
13 Main rail
14 Pin rail
15 Chock rail
16 Belaying pins
17 Topgallant forecastle deck

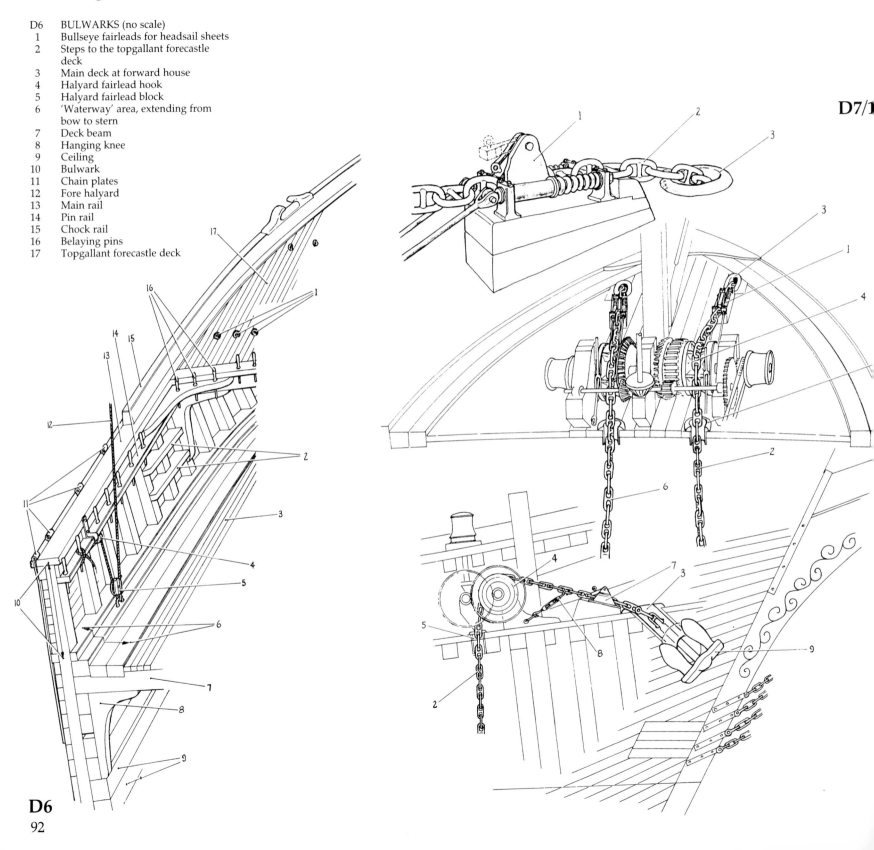

D6

D7/1 *Anchor chains, chain stoppers, hawse*
Spring-loaded riding stopper, starboard side
Anchor chain, starboard
Inboard end of hawse pipe, starboard
Wildcat (within the windlass assembly), starboard
Chain port, starboard
Anchor chain, port
Riding stopper, common (not spring-loaded) type
Stockless bow anchor (drawn up into the hawse pipe)

D7/2 *Bow anchors*
Shackle
Crown
Flukes

The *Bertha L. Downs* carried stockless bow anchors, port and starboard, weighing 4090 lbs. and 4070 lbs. respectively, according to her launching coverge in the *Bath Anvil* newspaper. These were manufactured by the Baldt Anchor and Chain Corporation of Chester, Pennsylvania. These stockless anchors were raised by the vessel's engine-powered windlass and were drawn snugly into the hawse pipes with just the flukes and the crowns protruding.

The plane views of these Baldt stockless anchors are traced from Baldt catalog graphics sent by Capt. Douglas K. Lee which depict the 4000 lb. stockless anchors furnished for the six-master *Cora F. Cressy*. The stockless anchor models were similar. The linear dimensions shown here are approximate and relate to stockless anchors of the 4000 lb. range.

The *Bertha L. Downs* would also have been equipped with a 1250 lb. stream anchor and a 650 lb. kedge as noted in the specifications for similar schooners launched in Bath, Maine shipyards during WWI. These are 'old fashioned' stock anchors with fixed wooden, composite, or folding iron stocks probably handled from the deck with masthead fish tackles. Exact dimensions are unknown.

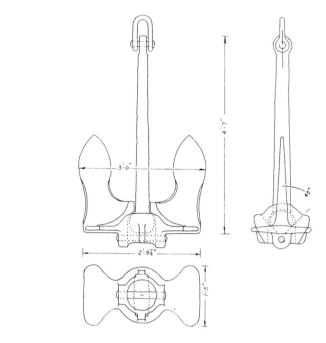

D7/2

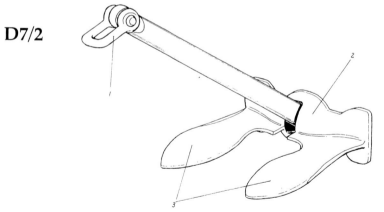

E Masts and spars

E1   BOWSPRIT (scale ⅛ inch = 1 foot)

E1/1   Bowsprit (yellow pine)
E1/2   Jibboom (Oregon pine)
E1/3   Boom for jib (spruce)
E1/4   Martingale (white oak)

NB   In section E, circled numbers on drawings refer to items of ironwork — see E6–E16.

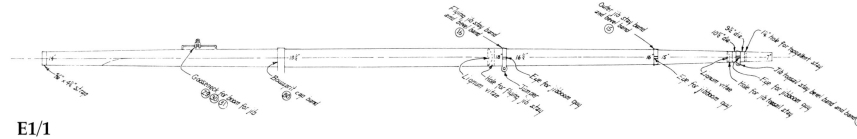

E1/1

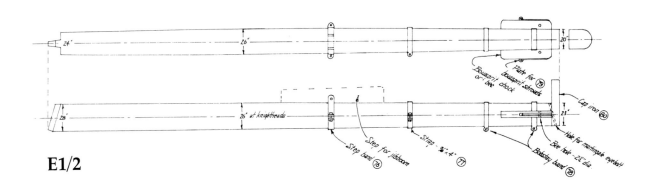

E1/2

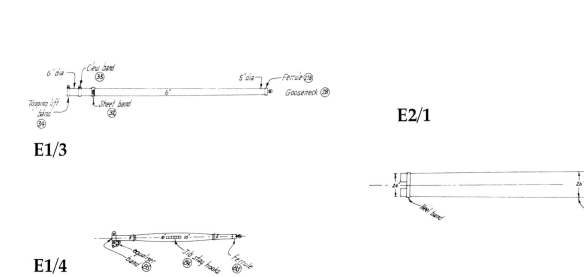

E1/3

E1/4

E2/1

Mast lengths: Foremast —   93'-0" (as drawn)
             Mainmast —   93'-2"
             Mizzen —   93'-6"
             Spanker —   93'-9"

             (All are Oregon pine)

Diameters: Main, Mizzen, Spanker masts —
             23" dia. at step
             25" dia. at mid length and partners
             23" dia. at hounds
             17" square at hounds
             16" square at head

2 LOWER MASTS

2/1 *Lower masts (lower fore mast shown)*
(Oregon pine) (scale ⅛ inch = 1 foot)
2/2 *Squared section of the masts at doubling*
(no scale)
2/3 *Saddles (white oak) (no scale)*
2/4 *Saddle band (no scale)*
2/5 *Cleats (white oak) (no scale)*

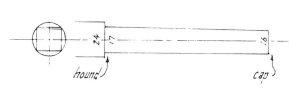

Port and starb'd sides taper inward ½" from hound to cap.
Aft side tapers 1".
Forward side has no taper. Cut parallel to mast ₵.

hound   cap

E2/2

E2/3

26" dia.- foremast
25" dia - main, mizzen, spanker

E2/4

E2/5

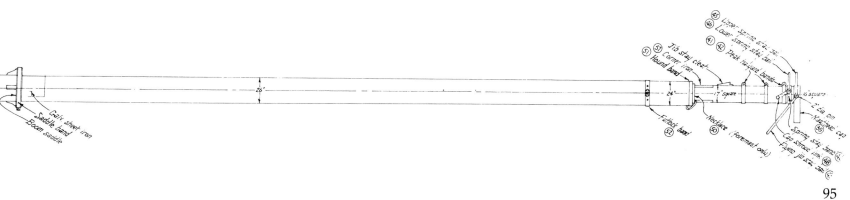

E Masts and spars

E3   TOPMASTS (scale ⅛ inch = 1 foot)

E3/1   Fore topmast (Oregon pine)

*E3/2   Main, mizzen and spanker topmasts
(spruce)*

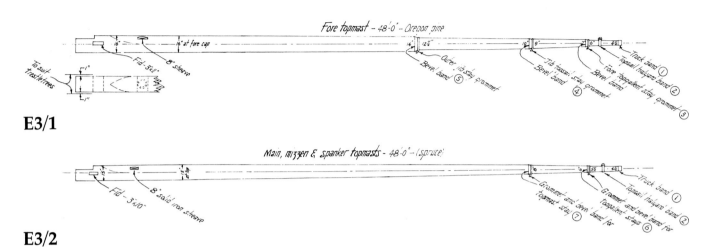

E3/1

E3/2

E4   GAFFS AND BOOMS

*E4/1   Fore, main and mizzen gaffs (spruce)
(scale ⅛ inch = 1 foot)*

*E4/2   Spanker gaff (spruce) (scale ⅛ inch = 1
foot)*

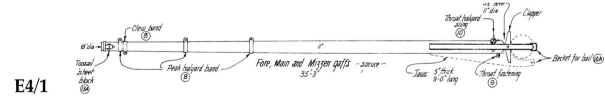

E4/1

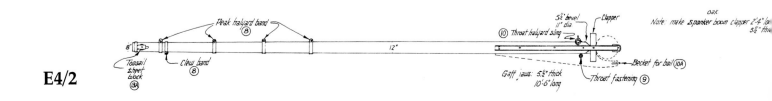

E4/2

E4/3

E4/4

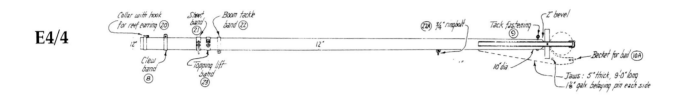

E4/5

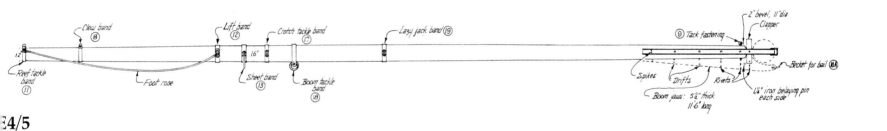

E4/6

E4/7

Note: make *spanker* boom clapper 2'-4" long
5½" thick

E Masts and spars

E5   TOPMAST STEP (scale ½ inch = 1 foot)

E5/1   *Elevation, starboard side and aft side*
E5/2   *Section at cap*
E5/3   *Section at trestletrees*
E5/4   *Section at hound band*

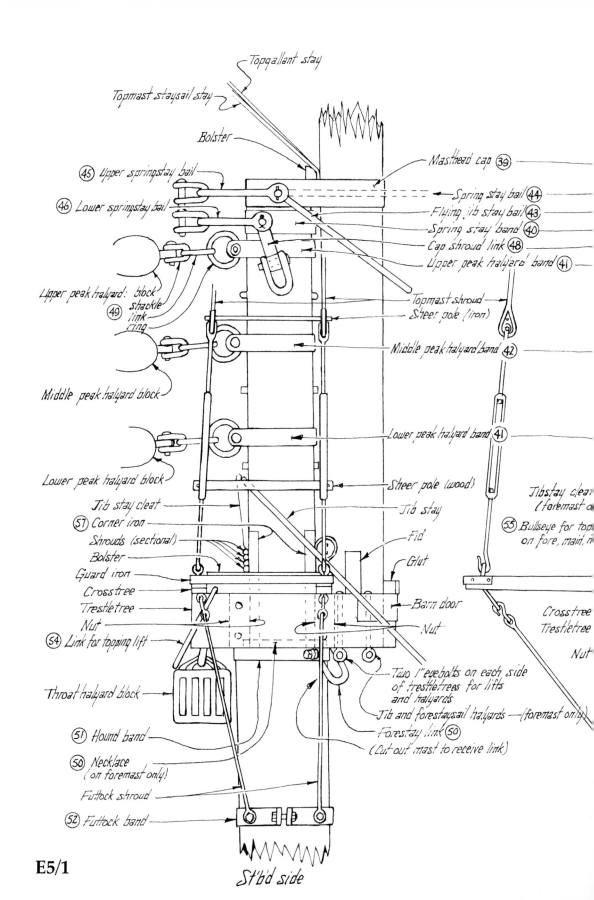

Topgallant stay

Topmast staysail stay

Bolster

㊺ Upper springstay bail

㊻ Lower springstay bail

Upper peak halyard: block
shackle
㊾ link
ring

Middle peak halyard block

Lower peak halyard block

Jib stay cleat

㊿ Corner iron

Shrouds (sectional)

Bolster

Guard iron

Crosstree

Trestletree

Nut

�54 Link for topping lift

Throat halyard block

�51 Hound band

�50 Necklace
(on foremast only)

Futtock shroud

�52 Futtock band

Masthead cap ㊴

Spring stay bail ㊹

Flying jib stay bail ㊸

Spring stay band ㊵

Cap shroud link ㊽

Upper peak halyard band ㊶

Topmast shroud

Sheer pole (iron)

Middle peak halyard band ㊷

Lower peak halyard band ㊶

Sheer pole (wood)

Jib stay

Fid

Glut

Barn door

Nut

Two 1" eyebolts on each side
of trestletrees for lifts
and halyards

Jib and forestaysail halyards — (foremast only)

Forestay link ㊿
(Cut out mast to receive link)

Jibstay clear
(foremast o

(55) Bullseye for top
on fore, main, r

Crosstree
Trestletree

Nut

E5/1

St'b'd side

98

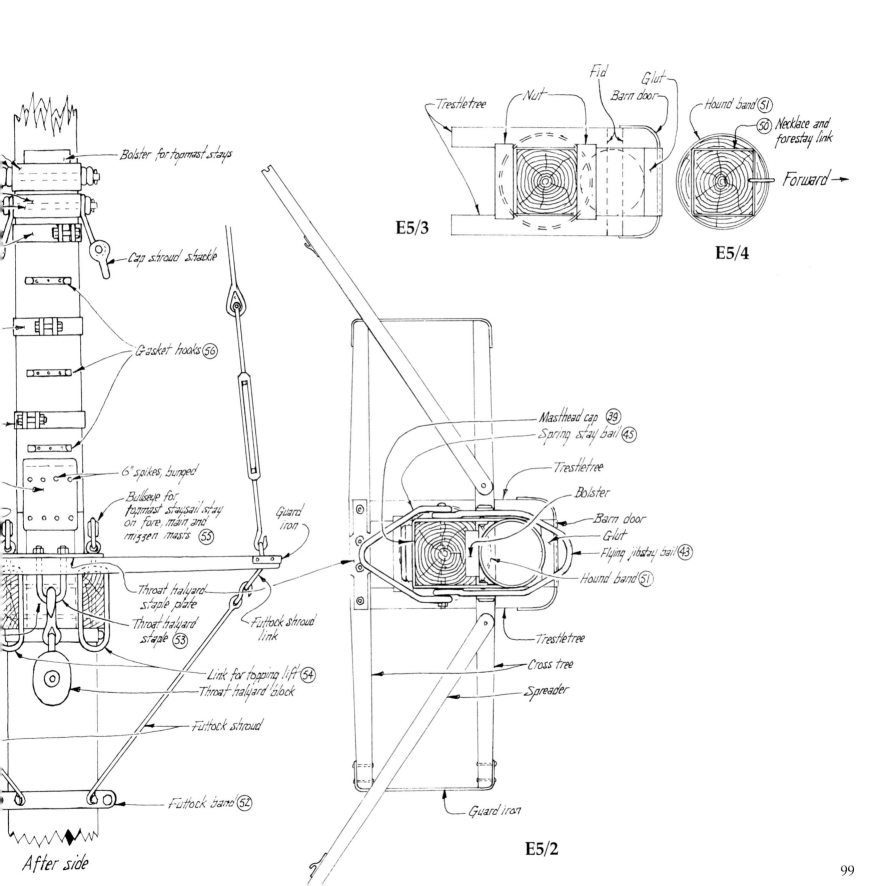

Bolster for topmast stays

Cap shroud shackle

Gasket hooks (56)

6" spikes, bunged

Bullseye for topmast staysail stay on fore, main and mizzen masts (55)

Throat halyard staple plate

Throat halyard staple (53)

Guard iron

Futtock shroud link

Link for topping lift (54)
Throat halyard block

Futtock shroud

Futtock band (52)

After side

Trestletree

Nut

Fid

Glut
Barn door

Hound band (51)

(50) Necklace and forestay link

Forward →

E5/3

E5/4

Masthead cap (39)
Spring stay bail (45)

Trestletree

Bolster

Barn door

Glut

Flying jibstay bail (43)

Hound band (51)

Trestletree

Cross tree

Spreader

Guard iron

E5/2

99

E Masts and spars

E5/5 Spreaders (white oak) (2 per mast)
E5/6 Crosstrees for the forward sides of all masts (white oak)
E5/7 Crosstrees for the aft sides of all masts (white oak)
E5/8 Trestletrees (yellow pine) (2 per mast–mirror duplicates)
E5/9 Nuts (yellow pine) (2 per mast)
E5/10 Glut (yellow pine) (1 per mast)
E5/11 Fid (oak) (1 per mast)
E5/12 Shroud bolster (oak) (2 per mast)

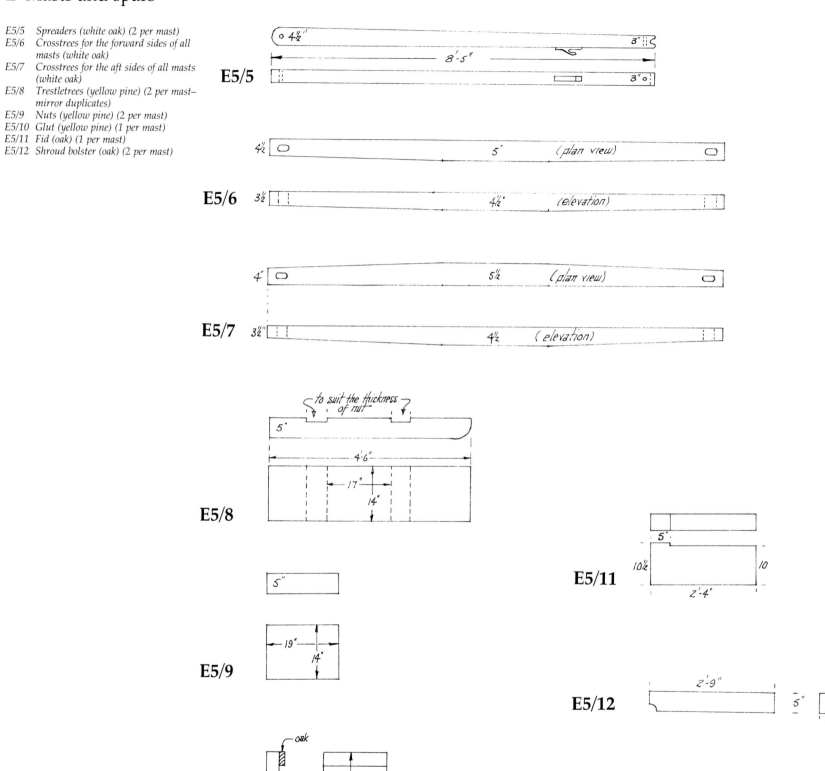

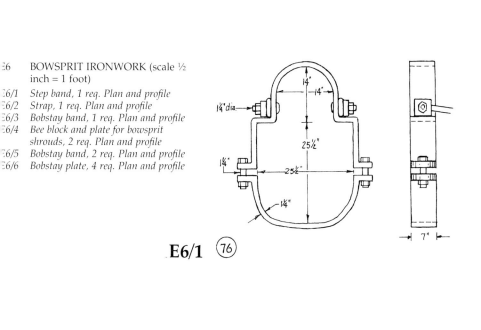

E6/1 ⑦⑥

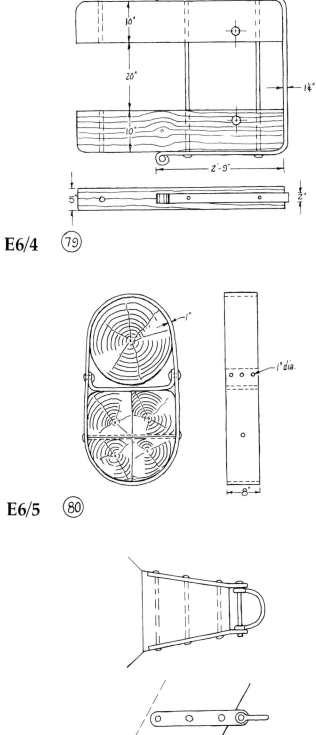

E6/4 ⑦⑨

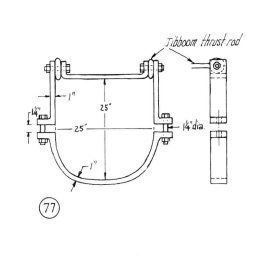

E6/2 ⑦⑦

E6/5 ⑧⓪

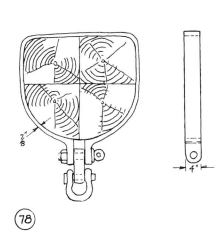

E6/3 ⑦⑧

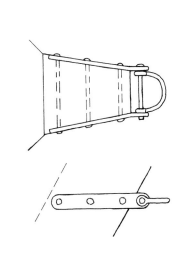

E6/6 ⑧②

101

E Masts and spars

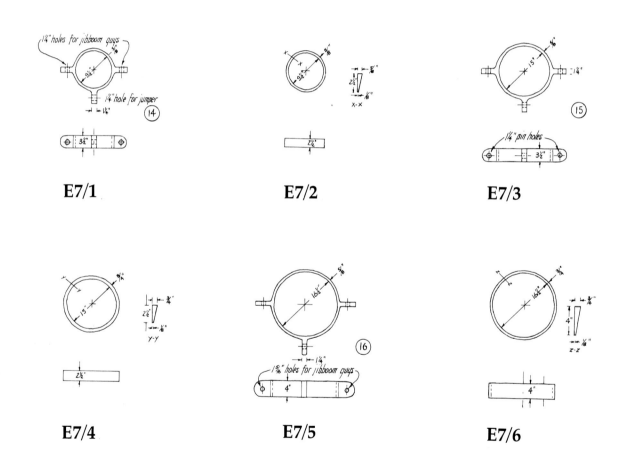

E7/1   **E7/2**   **E7/3**

E7/4   **E7/5**   **E7/6**

E8 BOOM FOR JIB, IRONWORK
(no scale)

E8/1 Sheet band, plan and profile
E8/2 Clew band (topping lift band similar),
plan and profile
E8/3 Arrangement of ironwork
1 Gooseneck
2 Sliding gunter
3 Guide bar
4 Guide bar eye
5 Gooseneck eye bolt

E9 MARTINGALE IRONWORK (scale
1 inch = 1 foot)

E9/1 Ferrule and eyebolt, 1 req.
E9/2 Jib stay hooks, 2 req. Plan and profile
E9/3 Equaliser and band, 1 req. Plan and
profile

E8/1

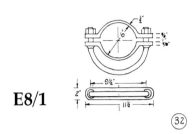

E9/1 ⑧⑶

E8/2

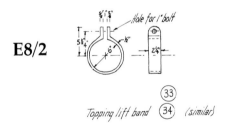

Topping lift band ㉞ (similar)

E9/2 ⑧⑷

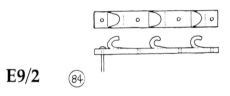

E8/3

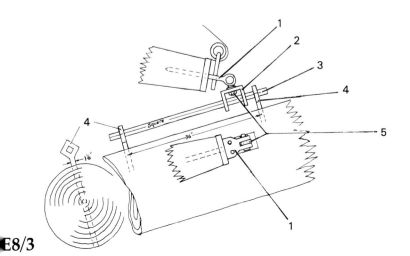

E9/3 ⑧⑸

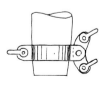

E Masts and spars

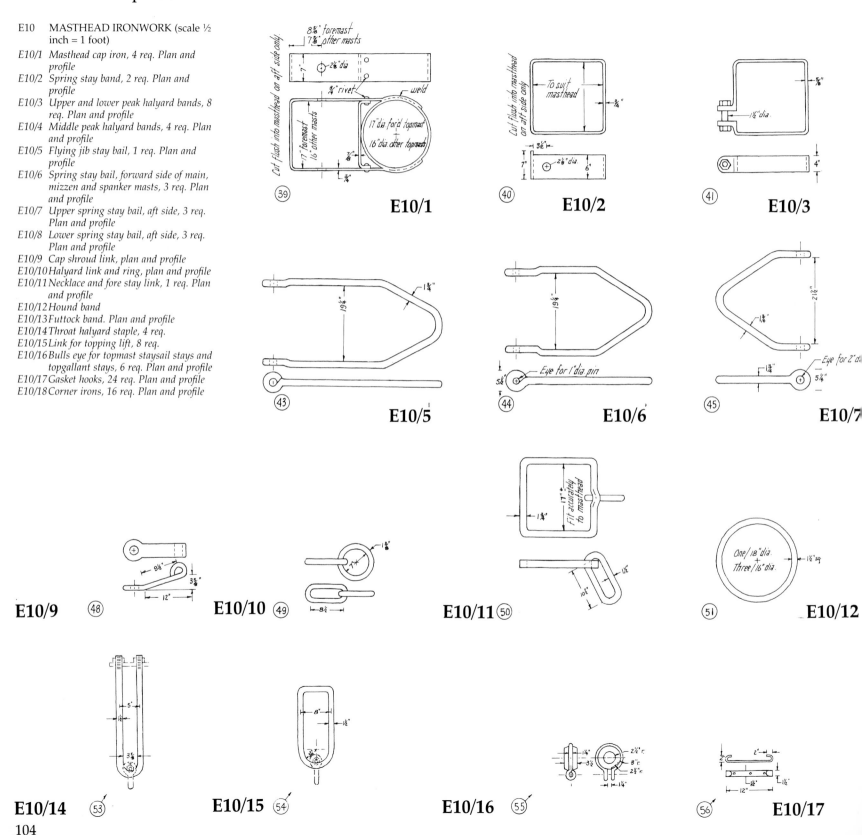

E10/1

E10/2

E10/3

E10/5

E10/6

E10/7

E10/9

E10/10

E10/11

E10/12

E10/14

E10/15

E10/16

E10/17

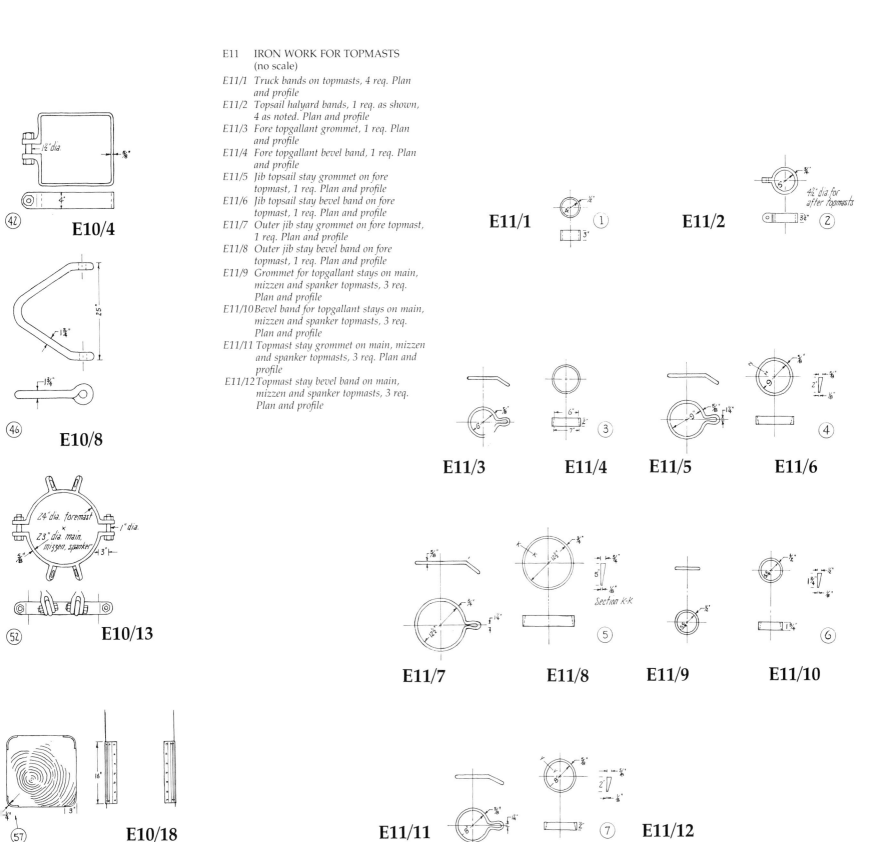

E10/4

E10/8

E10/13

E10/18

E11 IRON WORK FOR TOPMASTS
(no scale)

E11/1 Truck bands on topmasts, 4 req. Plan and profile

E11/2 Topsail halyard bands, 1 req. as shown, 4 as noted. Plan and profile

E11/3 Fore topgallant grommet, 1 req. Plan and profile

E11/4 Fore topgallant bevel band, 1 req. Plan and profile

E11/5 Jib topsail stay grommet on fore topmast, 1 req. Plan and profile

E11/6 Jib topsail stay bevel band on fore topmast, 1 req. Plan and profile

E11/7 Outer jib stay grommet on fore topmast, 1 req. Plan and profile

E11/8 Outer jib stay bevel band on fore topmast, 1 req. Plan and profile

E11/9 Grommet for topgallant stays on main, mizzen and spanker topmasts, 3 req. Plan and profile

E11/10 Bevel band for topgallant stays on main, mizzen and spanker topmasts, 3 req. Plan and profile

E11/11 Topmast stay grommet on main, mizzen and spanker topmasts, 3 req. Plan and profile

E11/12 Topmast stay bevel band on main, mizzen and spanker topmasts, 3 req. Plan and profile

E11/1

E11/2

E11/3

E11/4

E11/5

E11/6

E11/7

E11/8

E11/9

E11/10

E11/11

E11/12

E12 IRONWORK FOR GAFFS (no scale)

E12/1 *Peak halyard and clew band on gaffs and booms. Plan and profile*

E12/2 *Tack fastening on booms and gaffs, detail. 8 sets req. Plan and profile*

E12/3 *Throat halyard sling on gaffs, detail. 1 req. on spanker gaff, 3 on other gaffs. Plan and profile*

E12/4 *Gaff jaws ironwork*

1 Jaw

2 Becket for bail, 16 req.

3 Bail for gaff or boom, 8 req.

4 Gaff bail chip, 4 req.

E12/5 *Topsail sheet block, plan and profile*

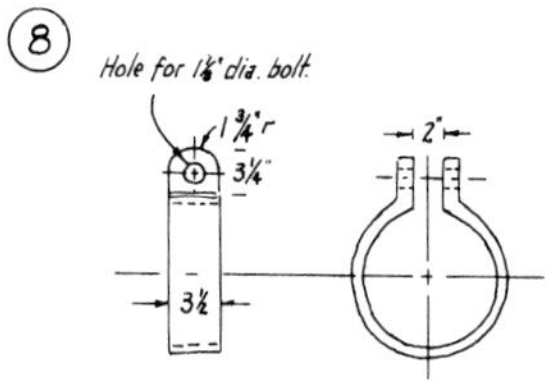
8
Hole for 1⅛" dia. bolt
1¾" r
3¼"
2"
3½

No. req'd.	Spanker gaff	
1 –	Outer peak halliard band	8¼"
1 –	2nd " " "	9½"
1 –	3rd " " "	10½"
1 –	4th " " "	11"
1 –	Clew band – –	8½" × 4" wide
	Fore, Main and Mizzen gaffs	
3 –	Outer peak halliard band	7¾"
3 –	2nd " " "	9¼"
3 –	3rd " " "	10½"
3 –	Clew band – —	7¾"
1 –	Clew band on spanker boom	13½ x 4" wide
3 –	" " " other booms	12" x 5½" wide

E12/1

E12/2

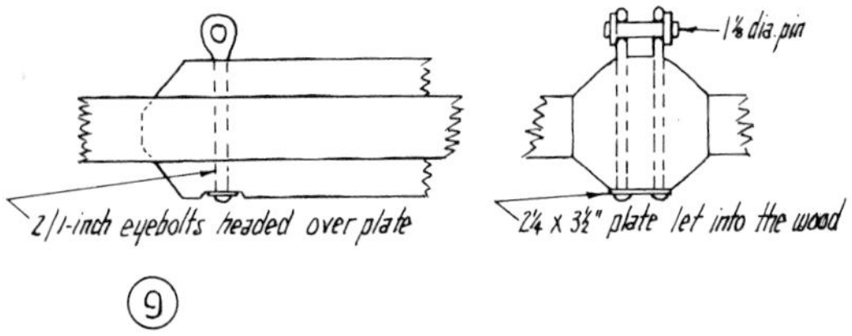
1⅛ dia. pin
2/1-inch eyebolts headed over plate
2¼ x 3½" plate let into the wood
9

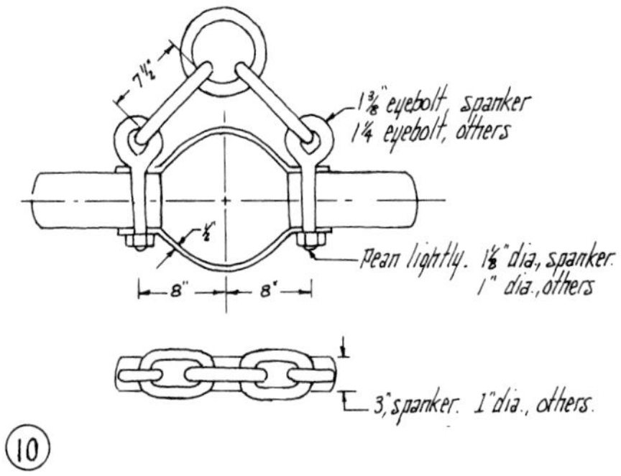
7½"
1⅜" eyebolt, spanker
1¼ eyebolt, others
Pean lightly. 1⅛" dia, spanker.
1" dia., others
8"
8"
3, spanker. 1" dia., others.
10

E12/3

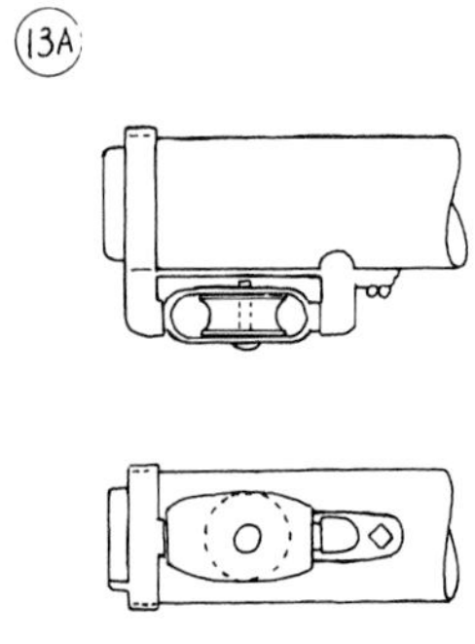
13A

E12/5

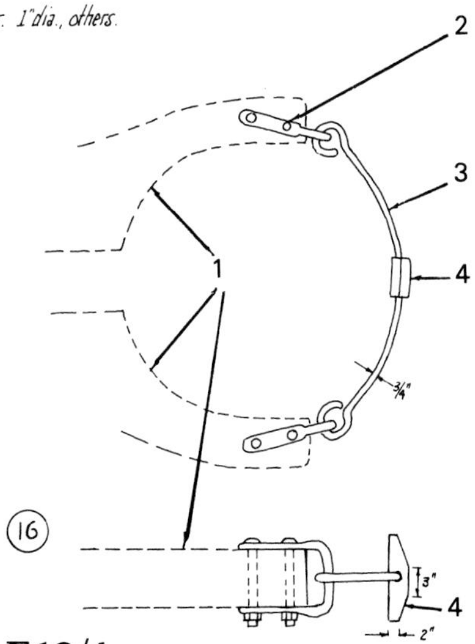
2
3
1
4
¾"
16
3"
4
2"

E12/4

E13 IRONWORK FOR SPANKER BOOM (scale ½ inch = 1 foot)

E13/1 *Reef tackle band, 1 req. Plan and profile*

E13/2 *Lift band, 1 req. Plan and profile*

E13/3 *Sheet band, 1 req. Plan and profile*

E13/4 *Crotch tackle band, 1 req. Plan and profile*

E13/5 *Boom tackle band, 1 req. Plan and profile*

E13/6 *Lazy jack band, 1 req. Plan and profile*

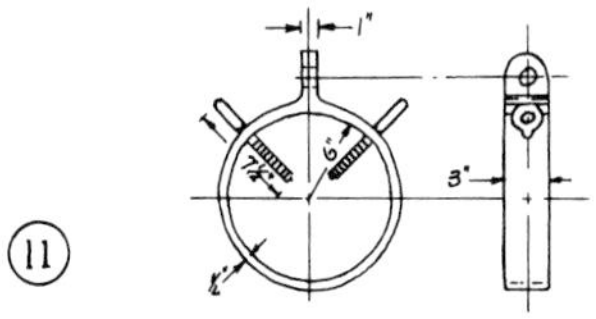
1"
6"
3"
11

E13/1

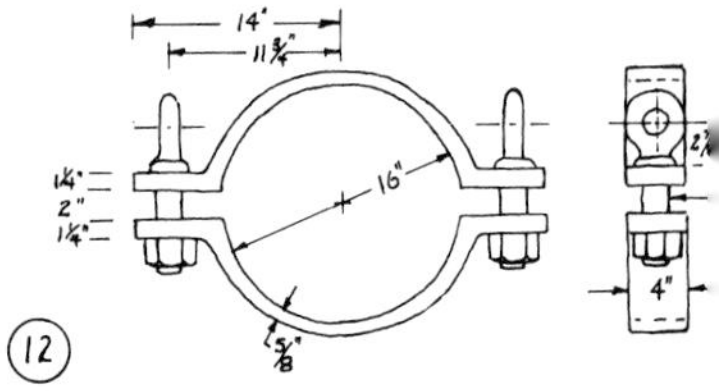
14"
11¾"
16"
4"
12

E13/2

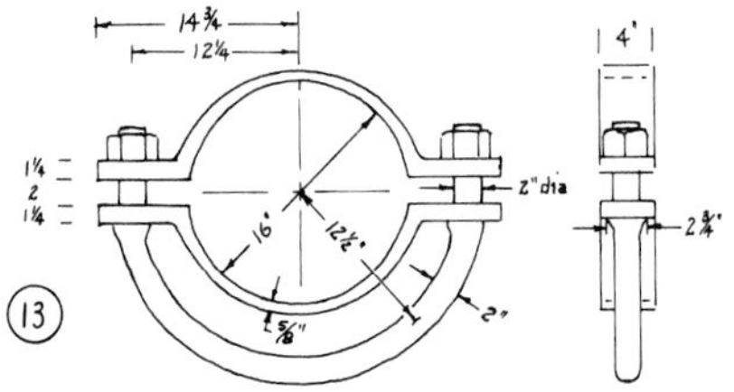
14¾
12¼
4"
2" dia
16"
12½"
2"
13

E13/3

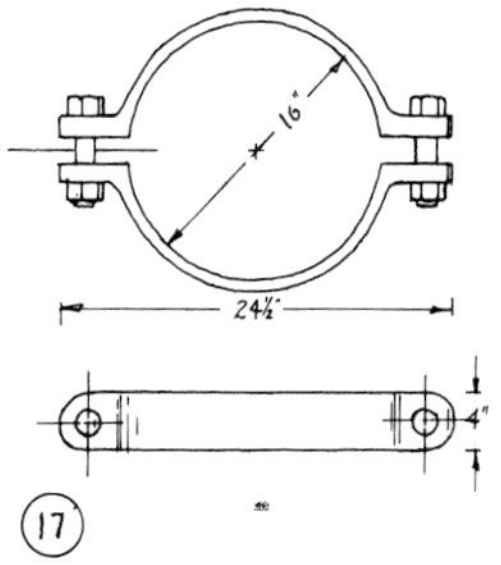
16"
24½"
4"
17

E13/4

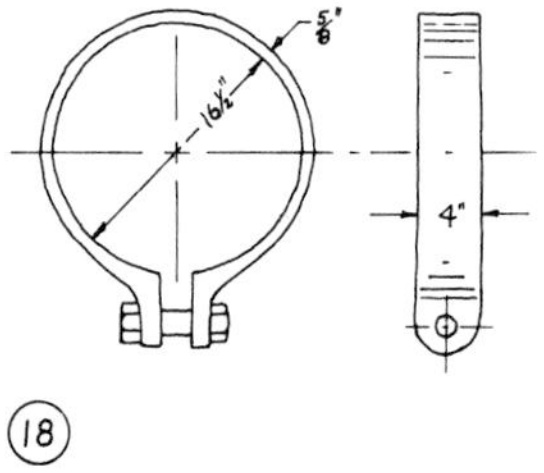
16½"
4"
18

E13/5

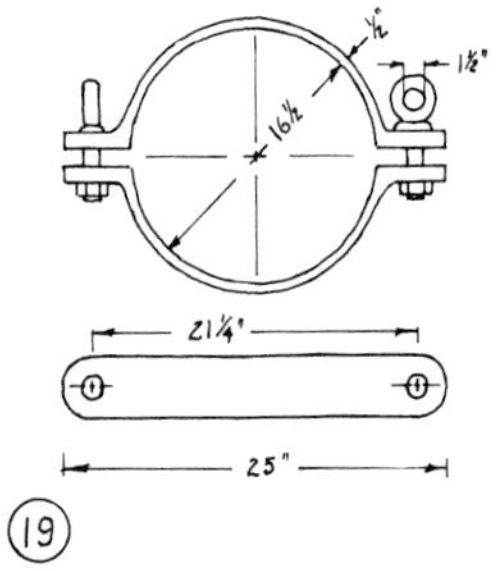
16½
1½"
21¼"
25"
19

E13/6

E14 IRONWORK FOR FORE, MAIN
AND MIZZEN BOOMS (scale ½
inch = 1 foot)

*E14/1 Collar with hook for reef earring, plan
and profile*
E14/2 Sheet bands, 3 req. Plan and profile
E14/3 Boom tackle band, plan and profile
E14/4 Ringbolt, 4 req.
E14/5 Topping lift band, plan and profile

E15 IRONWORK FOR STAYSAIL
BOOM (scale ½ inch = 1 foot)

*E15/1 Topping lift band, 1 req. Plan and
profile*
E15/2 Clew band, 1 req. Plan and profile
E15/3 Sheet band, 1 req. Plan and profile

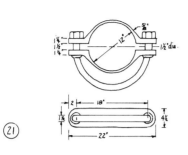

E14/1

E14/2

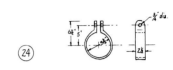

E15/1

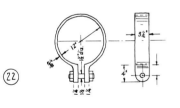

E14/3

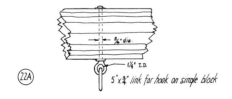

5"x¾" link for hook on simple block

E14/4

E15/2

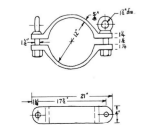

E14/5

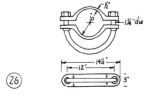

E15/3

E Masts and spars

E16   IRONWORK FOR FORESTAYSAIL
        BOOM (no scale)

E16/1 Arrangement of ironwork
1   Topping lift band
2   Clew band
3   Sheet band
4   Ferrule
5   Gooseneck
6   Forestaysail boom support
7   Forestaysail boom support step
8   Forestaysail boom support plate
9   Staple for gooseneck

E16/2 Clew band, plan and profile
E16/3 Support step
E16/4 Support plate

E16/1

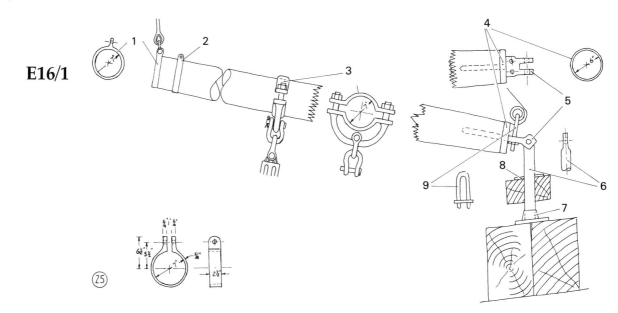

E16/2

E16/3

16/4

108

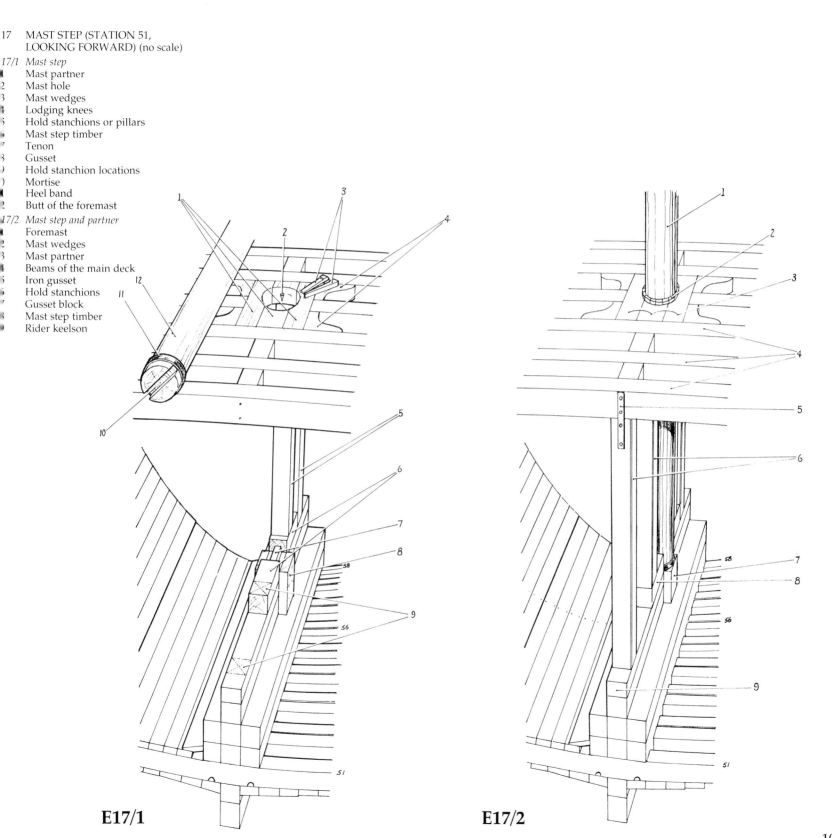

17 MAST STEP (STATION 51,
    LOOKING FORWARD) (no scale)

17/1 *Mast step*
1   Mast partner
2   Mast hole
3   Mast wedges
4   Lodging knees
5   Hold stanchions or pillars
6   Mast step timber
7   Tenon
8   Gusset
9   Hold stanchion locations
10   Mortise
11   Heel band
12   Butt of the foremast

17/2 *Mast step and partner*
1   Foremast
2   Mast wedges
3   Mast partner
4   Beams of the main deck
5   Iron gusset
6   Hold stanchions
7   Gusset block
8   Mast step timber
9   Rider keelson

E17/1   E17/2

F Rigging

F1 STANDING RIGGING

F1/1 Profile (scale ¹⁄₁₆ inch = 1 foot)

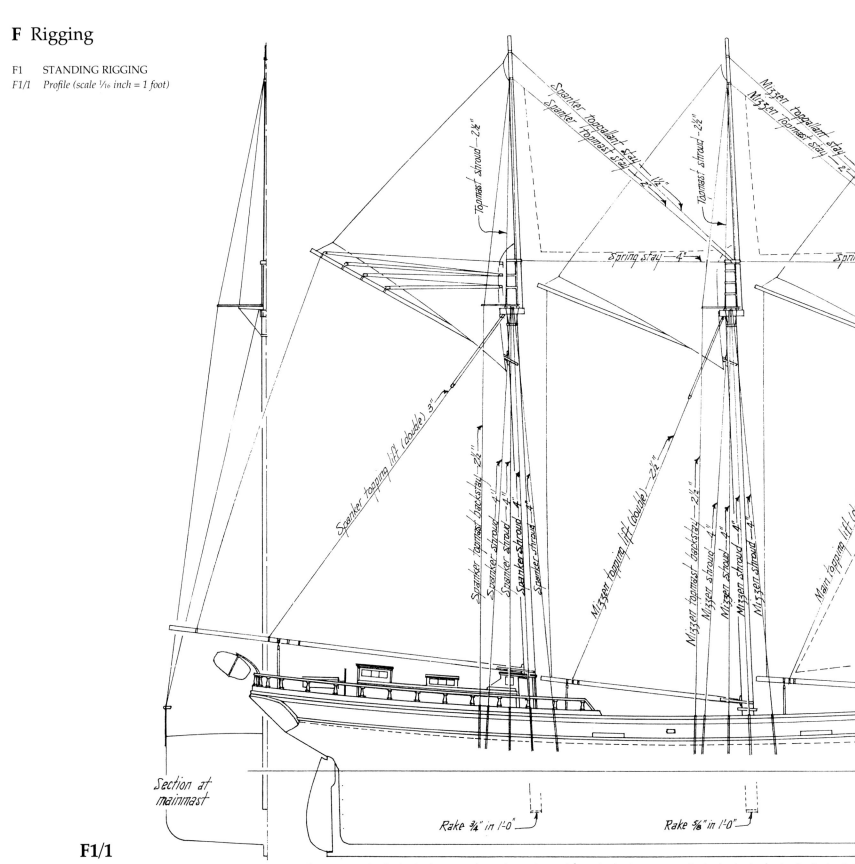

F1/1

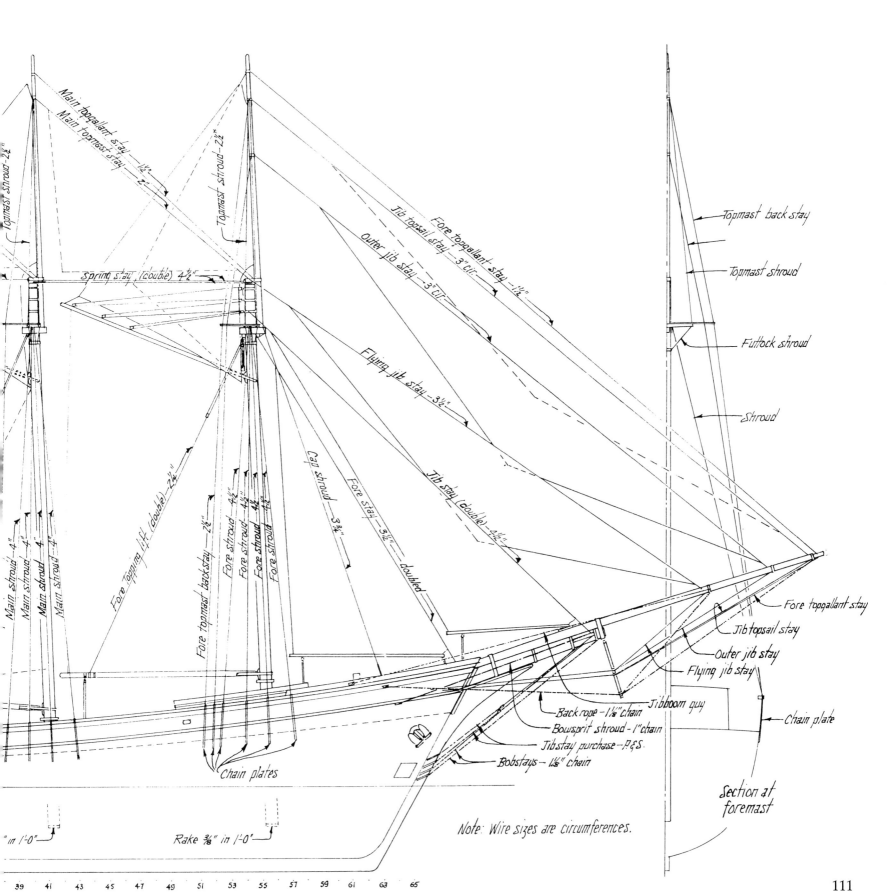

Topmast shroud — 2½"

Main topgallant stay — 1½"

Main topmast stay — 2"

Topmast shroud — 2½"

Spring stay (double) 4½"

Fore topgallant stay

Jib topsail stay — 3" cir.

Outer jib stay — 3" cir.

Flying jib stay — 3½"

Jib stay (double) — 4½"

Topmast back stay

Topmast shroud

Futtock shroud

Shroud

Fore topping lift (double) — 2½"

Main shroud — 4"
Main shroud — 4"
Main shroud — 4"
Main shroud — 4"

Fore topmast backstay — 2½"

Fore shroud 4½"
Fore shroud 4½"
Fore shroud 4½"
Fore shroud 4½"

Cap shroud — 3¾"

Fore stay — 3½" — doubled

Chain plates

Fore topgallant stay

Jib topsail stay

Outer jib stay

Flying jib stay

Jibboom guy

Chain plate

Back rope — 1⅛" chain

Bowsprit shroud — 1" chain

Jibstay purchase — P.&S.

Bobstays — 1⅛" chain

Chain plates

Section at foremast

Note: Wire sizes are circumferences.

" in 1'-0"

Rake ⅜" in 1'-0"

39   41   43   45   47   49   51   53   55   57   59   61   63   65

F Rigging

F1/2 Perspective view

Stays support the masts, bowsprit and jibboom in the fore and aft direction.

Shrouds support masts, bowsprit and jibboom in the athwartships direction. Shrouds serving one side of the vessel have counterparts on the other.

1   Fore topgallant stay
2   Jib topsail stay
3   Outer jib stay
4   Flying jib stay
5   Jib stay (double wire)
6   Fore stay
7   Outer jibboom guy
8   Inner jibboom guy
9   Outer martingale stay
10 Inner martingale stay
11 Bowsprit shroud
12 Cap shroud
13 Fore shrouds
14 Fore topmast preventer backstay
15 Fore topmast backstay
16 Main shrouds
17 Main topmast backstay
18 Mizzen shrouds
19 Mizzen topmast backstay
20 Spanker shrouds
21 Spanker topmast backstay
22 Spanker topmast stay
23 Spanker topgallant stay
24 Spring stay
25 Mizzen topmast stay
26 Mizzen topgallant stay
27 Topmast shrouds
28 Futtock shrouds
29 Upper spring stay
30 Lower spring stay
31 Main topmast stay
32 Main topgallant stay
33 Fore topmast preventer backstay

F1/2

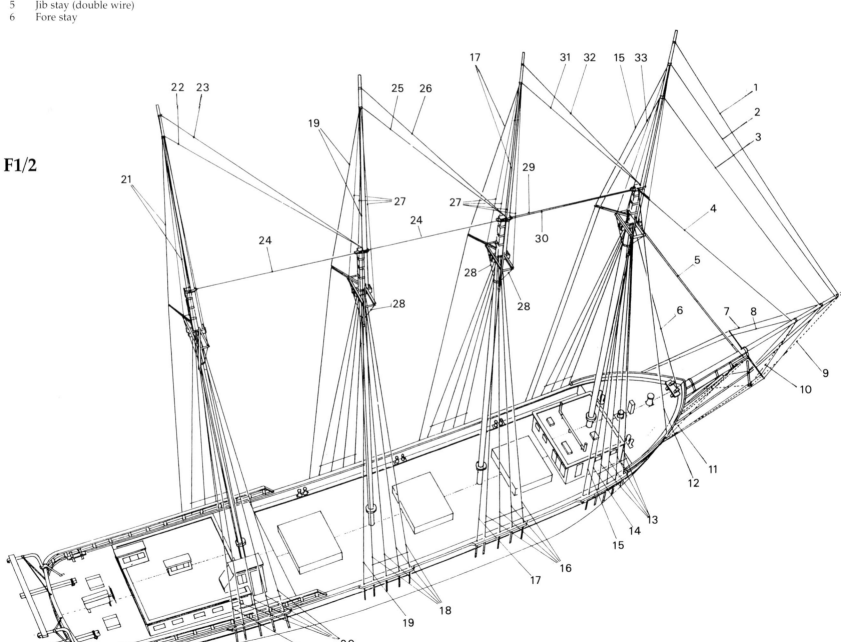

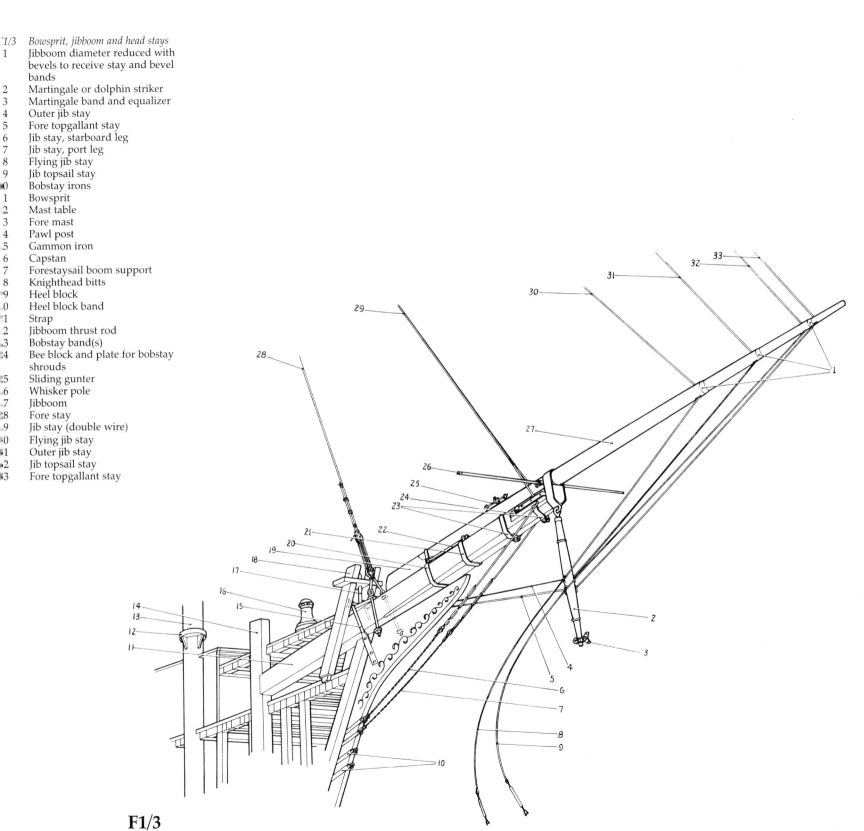

F1/3

F Rigging

F1/4   *Fore mast*
1   Fore topgallant stay
2   Jib topsail stay
3   Outer jib stay
4   Flying jib stay
5   Jib stay (double wire)
6   Fore stay
7   Outer jib stay
8   Fore topgallant stay
9   Jib topsail stay
10   Flying jib stay
11   Cap shroud
12   Fore shrouds
13   Fore topmast preventer backstay
14   Fore topmast backstay
15   Fore channel
16   Fore chain plates
17   Iron rod sheer pole
18   Wooden turnbuckle keeper
19   Futtock band
20   Futtock shroud
21   Trestle tree
22   Cross tree
23   Spreader
24   Spring stay
25   Lower spring stay
26   Upper spring stay
27   Main topgallant stay
28   Main topmast stay
29   Topmast shrouds
30   Fore topmast preventer backstay
31   Fore topmast backstay

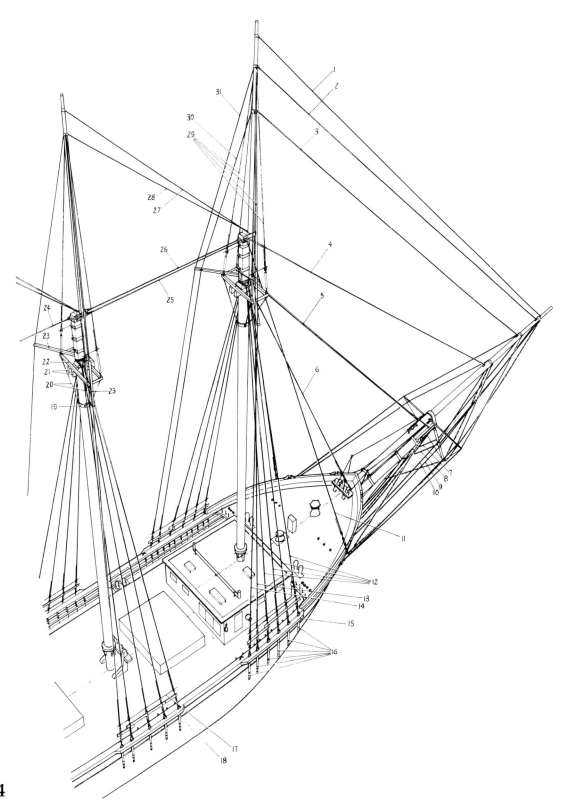

F1/4

F1/5 Fore mast and bowsprit
1   Outer jibboom guy
2   Inner jibboom guy
3   Whisker pole
4   Flying jib stay
5   Outer jib stay
6   Jib topsail stay
7   Fore topgallant stay
8   Whisker guy
9   Martingale
10 Inner martingale stay
11 Outer martingale stay
12 Equalizer
13 Bee block, port and starboard
14 Martingale back stay
15 Bowsprit shroud, port and starboard
16 Jib stay, starboard leg
17 Jib stay, port leg
18 Inner bob stay

19 Outer bob stay
20 Cap stay chain plate, port and
    starboard
21 Timber port, port and starboard
22 Chain plates for fore shrouds, port
    and starboard
23 Chain plates for fore topmast
    backstays, port and starboard
24 Fore channel, port and starboard

25 Turnbuckle keeper
26 Sheer pole
27 Ratlines
28 Fore topmast backstay
29 Fore topmast lower backstay
30 Fore shrouds
31 Foremast
32 Cap stay, port and starboard
33 Fore stay

34 Boom for staysail
35 Boom for jib
36 Bowsprit
37 Jibboom
38 Jib stay (double wire)
39 Flying jib stay
40 Outer jib stay
41 Jib topsail stay
42 Fore topgallant stay

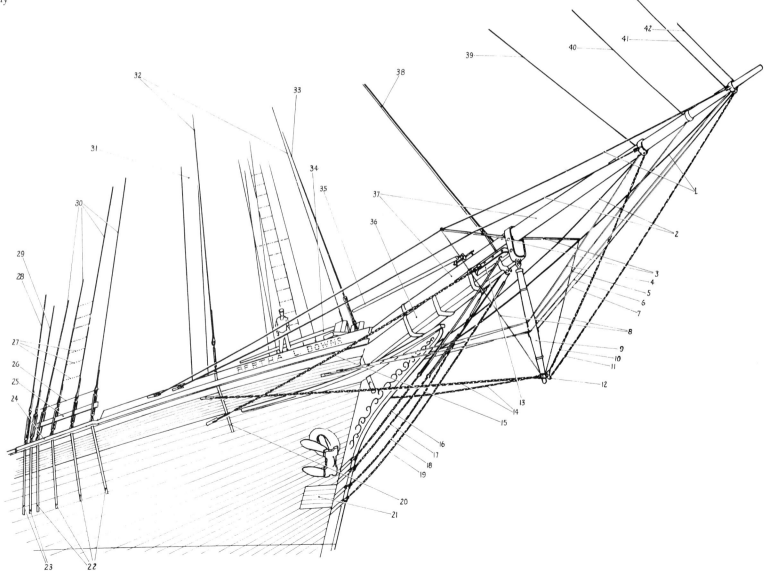

F1/5

115

F Rigging

F1/6   *Tack of the forestaysail boom*
1   Jib stay
2   Jibboom
3   Cap iron
4   Whisker pole
5   Sliding gunter
6   Plate for bowsprit shroud
7   Jib stay
8   Bowsprit
9   Bobstay band
10   Jibboom thrust rod
11   Jibboom heel iron
12   Step band

F1/7   *Sheet-block horse*
F1/8   *Chainplate shackle for shroud*
F1/9   *Chainplate shackle for backstay*

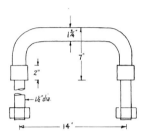

F1/7

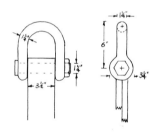

F1/8

13   Knighthead bitts
14   Chock rail
15   Cover board
16   Forestaysail boom support
17   Forestaysail boom gooseneck
18   Tack tiedown staple
19   Belaying pins for headsail
     downhauls
20   Forestaysail boom
21   Deadeye in lieu of turnbuckle (for
     tightening this particular stay)
22   Forestaysail slacking line
23   Forestaysail bolt rope
24   Forestaysail
25   Fore stay

F1/6

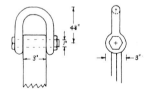

F1/9

F2   RUNNING RIGGING

Running rigging is the collection of flexible lines (usually hemp or manila cordage) used to raise sails, lower sails, trim, reef, gather and furl sails, hoist and lower the yawl boat etc. All such lines bearing weight or strain were led to the powered gypsy heads in this class of schooner so that the heavy gear could be handled by a minimal number of crewmen.

F2/1   *Perspective view*

In *F2/1*, the yawl boat has been hoisted and the spanker raised by means of messenger lines extending the boat falls and the spanker halyards to the gypsy heads located on the port and starboard sides of the forward house. The hands have moved forward and are raising the mizzen.

Nine men are involved. Two men have unbelayed the throat and peak halyards, port and starboard, bent their ends to the mesenger lines, and are signalling 'hoist'. The engineer standing in the hoister doorway has thrown the clutch to activate the gypsies. Three men, each side, have taken wraps around the gypsies and are tailling the messengers as they come off the drums. The mizzen sail lies loose in the lazy jacks as it rises.

Hatches are battened and their strongbacks are bolted down. The dinghy is lashed down atop the after house, starboard side. Inboard of it are the gangplank and the reefing plank lashed together.

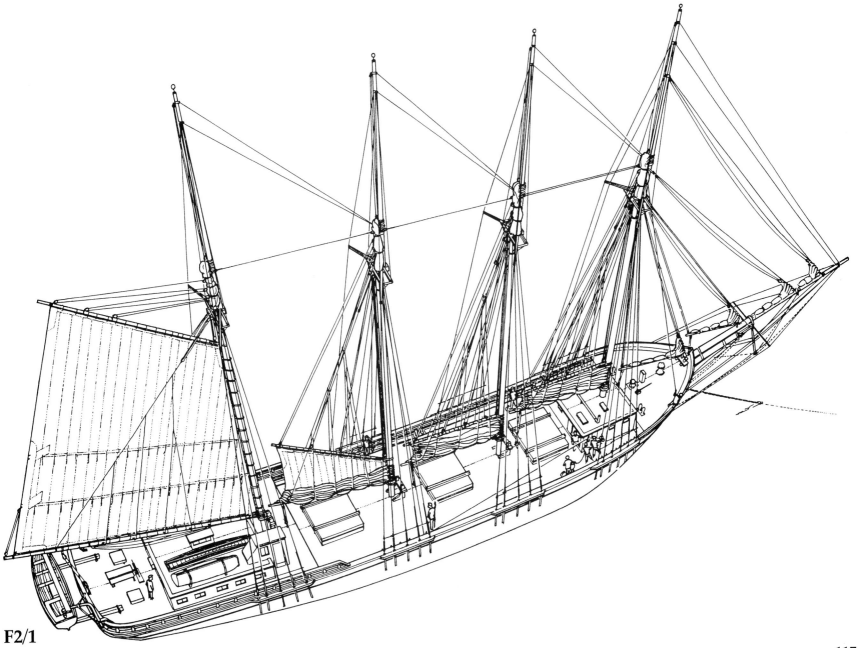

F2/1

F Rigging

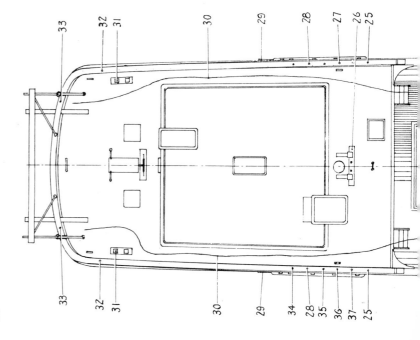

F2/2

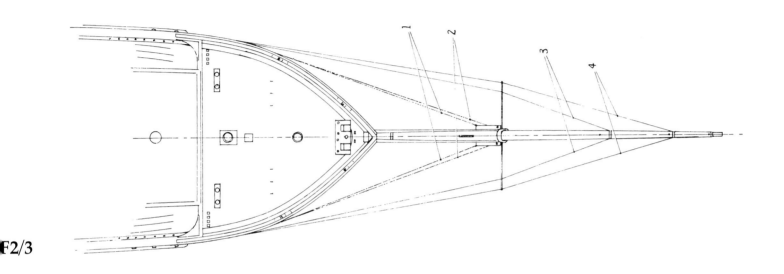

F2/3

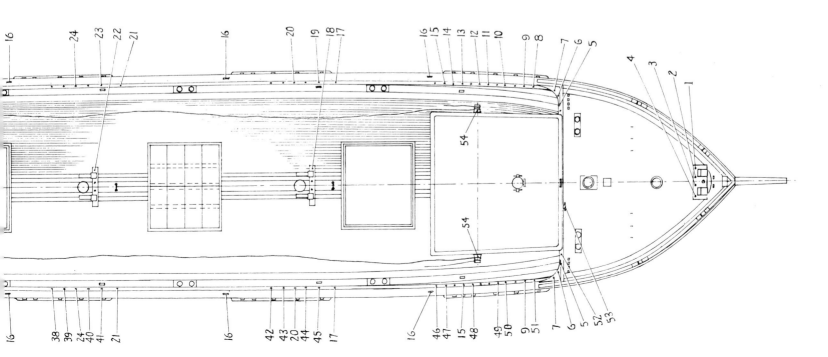

119

F Rigging

A gaff topsail is normally set to leeward of the halyards which support the gaff of the lower sail, but with the tack stretched taut over the windward side of the gaff.

A gaff topsail is *raised* by a halyard which runs through a block at the head of the topmast and belayed, usually, at the starboard pin rail. It is *sheeted* outward with a chain sheet run through a special cheek block at the end of the gaff and is chain-spliced to a manila tail rope before descending to the deck through a tail block under the gaff jaw. The tack of the topsail is stretched downward and forward by a tackline run directly to the lee pin rail across the forward side of the lower mast.

The *clew line* purses the topsail inward and lifts it clear of the gaff halyards, the spring stay and the topmast stays which block a gaff topsail from filling away on the opposite tack when the vessel comes about. Sheet and tackline must be shifted and re-set by a masthead hand as the topsail is clewed over these obstacles.

The clew line is dead-ended at the topsail's tack cringle. It courses outward and upward through a bullseye or dumb block stitched into the bunt of the topsail, thence to a block at the peak, through a fairlead block partway down the topsail's luff, then to the pinrail, starboard side. Sometimes the bullseye is not stitched, but toggled through the sail for strength. Sometimes, as pointed out by Capt. Biff Bowker, the clew line was led right through the sail via a heavy grommet and continued to the head block as before, but on the opposite side of the sail. Same effect.

'Most of our large American schooners had double topping lifts and lazyjacks. A lot of Canadian vessels had double lifts only on the spanker and single lifts on the others. You couldn't have lazyjacks with a single lift and many of those bluenosers were too cheap to put them on the spanker. That meant that many times the sails blew over the side when being lowered and had to be dragged back and rolled up on the booms by hand.' (*Capt. Biff Bowker, commentary on this drawing*)

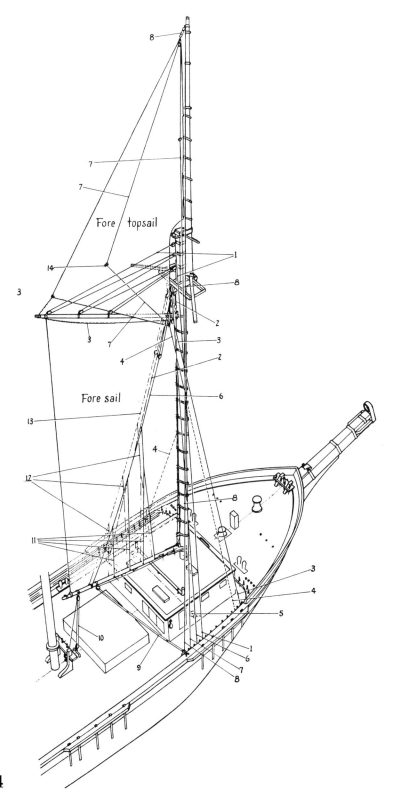

F2/4

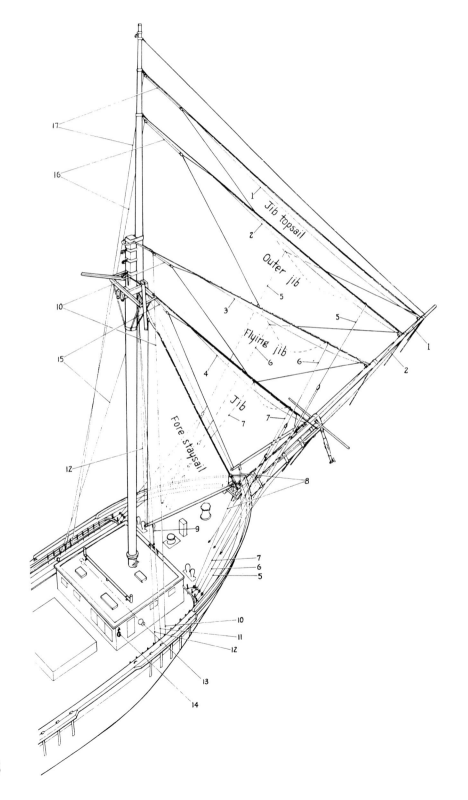

F2/5

G Sails

G1   PROFILE SAIL PLAN (scale ⅟₁₆ inch
      = 1 foot)

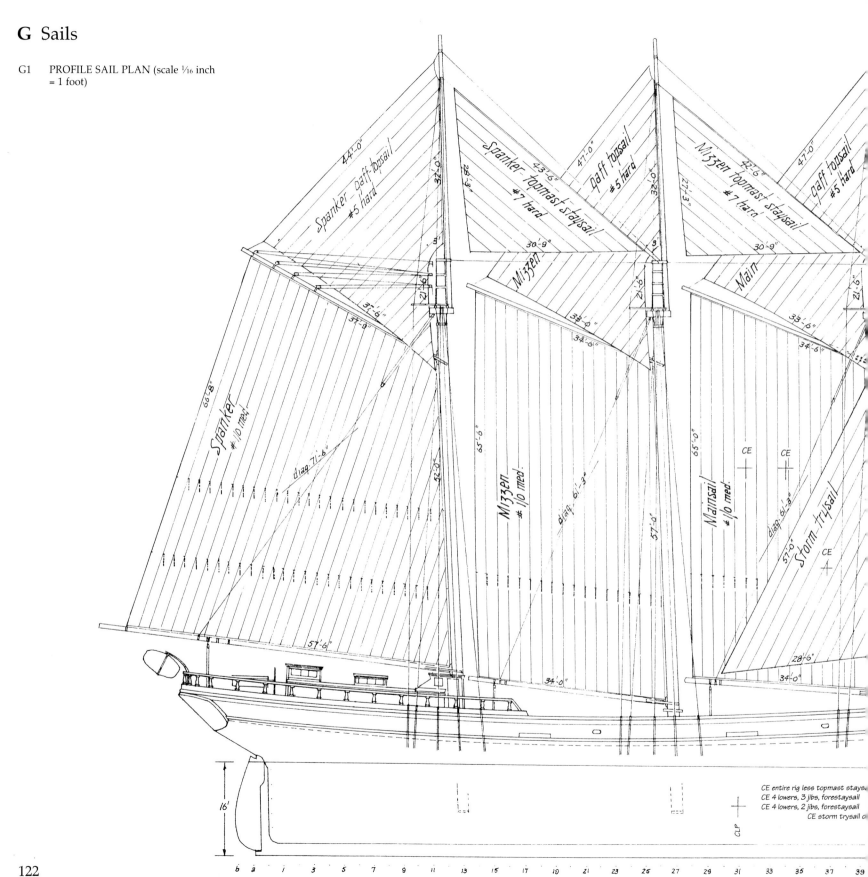

CE entire rig less topmast stays
CE 4 lowers, 3 jibs, forestaysail
CE 4 lowers, 2 jibs, forestaysail
CE storm trysail o

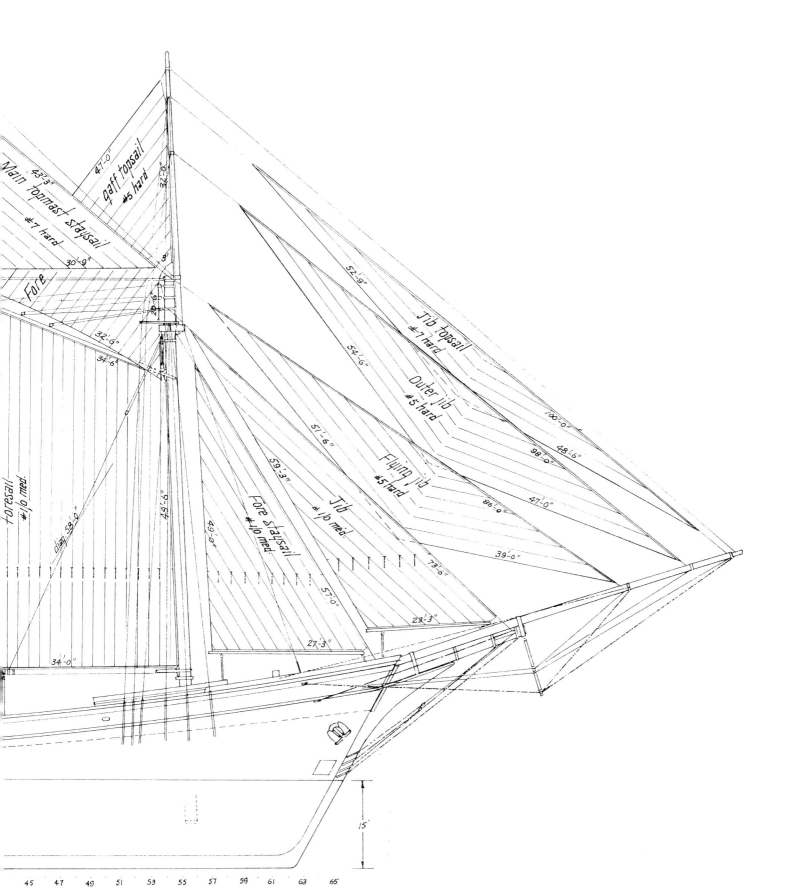

Gaff topsail
#5 hard
47'-0"
43'-3"
34'-0"

Main topmast staysail
#7 hard
30'-9"

Fore
32'-0"
34'-6"

Foresail
#10 med.
diam. 58'-0"
34'-0"

49'-6"

49'-0"

Fore staysail
#10 med.
57'-0"
27'-3"

Jib
#10 med.
59'-3"
57'-6"

Flying jib
#5 hard
73'-6"
23'-3"

Outer jib
#5 hard
54'-6"

Jib topsail
#7 hard
52'-9"

100'-0"
48'-6"
98'-0"
86'-0"
47'-0"
39'-0"

15'

45   47   49   51   53   55   57   59   61   63   65

123

G Sails

G2   JIB SAILS (scale ¹⁄₁₆ inch = 1 foot)
G2/1   *Jib topsail*
G2/2   *Outer jib*
G2/3   *Flying jib*
G2/4   *Jib*

G3   FOREMAST SAILS (scale ¹⁄₁₆ inch = 1 foot)
G3/1   *Fore staysail*
G3/2   *Foresail*
G3/3   *Fore gaff topsail*

G4   MAINMAST SAILS (scale ¹⁄₁₆ inch = 1 foot)
G4/1   *Main topmast staysail*
G4/2   *Main gaff topsail*
G4/3   *Mainsail*
G4/4   *Storm trysail*

G5   MIZZEN MAST SAILS (scale ¹⁄₁₆ inch = 1 foot)
G5/1   *Mizzen topmast staysail*
G5/2   *Mizzen gaff topsail*
G5/3   *Mizzen*

G6   SPANKER SAILS (scale ¹⁄₁₆ inch = 1 foot)
G6/1   *Spanker topmast staysail*
G6/2   *Spanker gaff topsail*
G6/3   *Spanker*

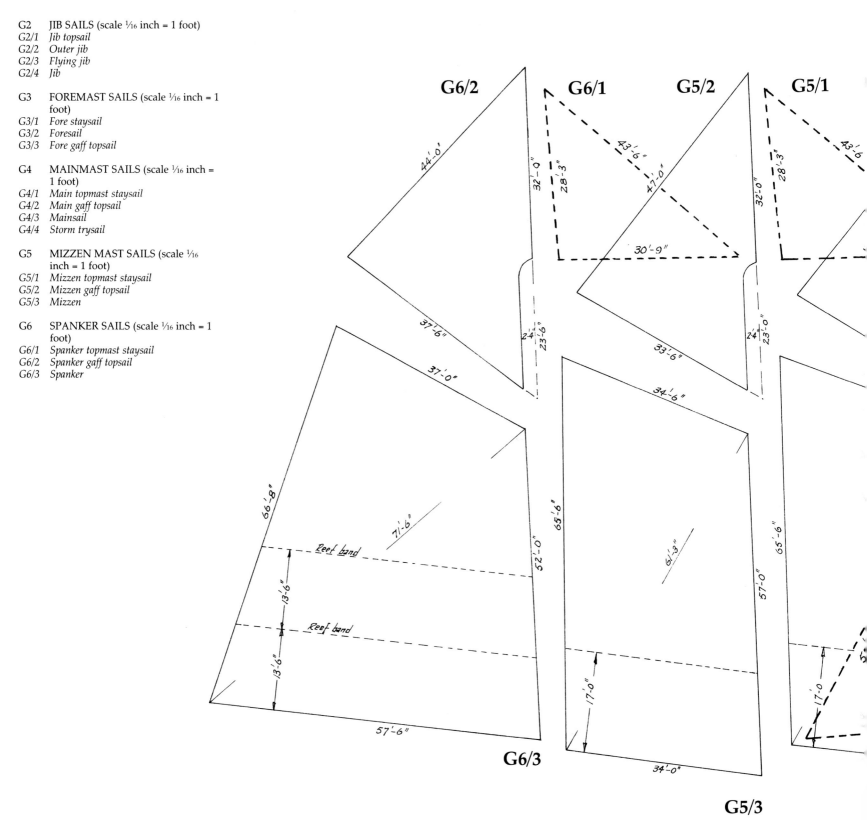

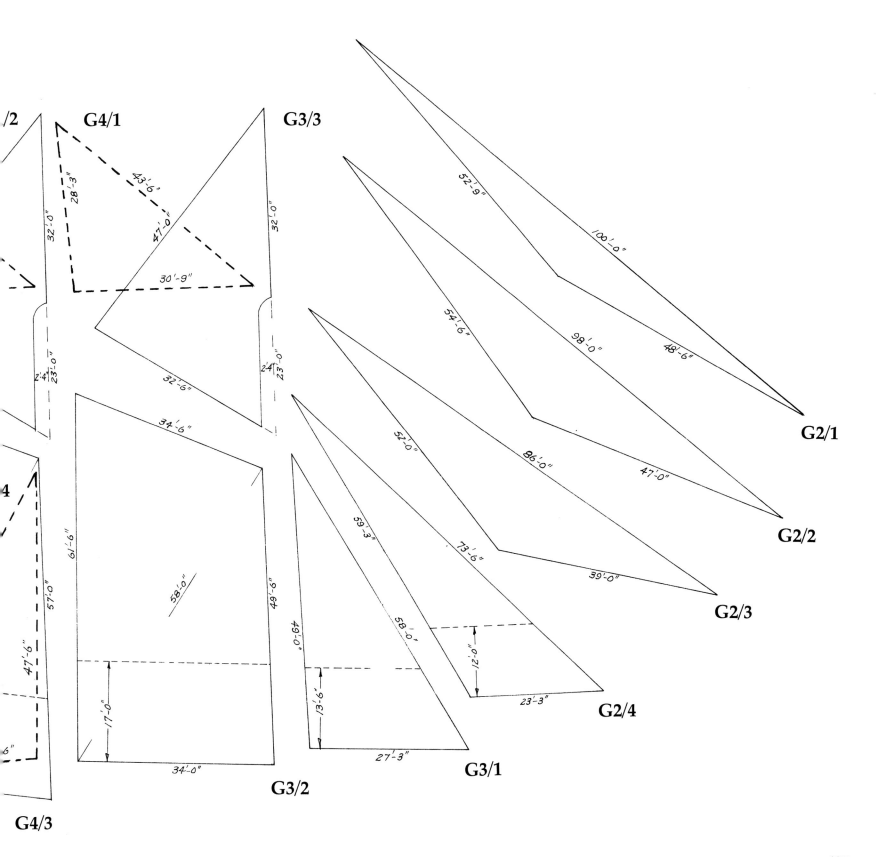

Wire Rigging Sizes

McComber,- Whyte Moon Co Rigging Wire

Jib stays	4½" circ	
Fore stay	3⅞" circ	double
Preventer masthead stays	4" "	
Flying jib stays	3½" "	
Jib topsail stay	3" "	
Fore topmast stay	2¼" "	
Fore topgallent stay	1½" "	
Main, mizzen, and spanker topmast stays	2" "	
" " " " topgallant stays	1½" "	
Foremast shrouds	4½" "	
Main, mizzen and spanker mast shrouds	4" "	
Topmast backstays	2½" "	
" shrouds	2½" "	
Spring stays, between fore and mainmast	4½" "	double
Balance of spring stays	4" "	
Jibboom guys	3" and 3½" circ	
Boom topping lifts – fore, main, mizzen	2½" "	
Spanker boom topping lifts	3" "	

Running Rigging

Throat and peak halyards, and anchor purchase	3¼" manila
Fore staysails, jib, and flying jib holds	2½" "
Spanker boom lifts, and boat tackles	2¾" "
Fore, main & mizzen boom lifts	2½" "
Boom tackles	3" "
Fore, main, mizzen and spanker sheets	3¾" "
Gaff top holds	2¼" "
Gaff top clewlines and reef tackles	2¼" "
Staysail holds	2" "
" clewlines	2" "
" sheets and deck tackles	2½" "
Gaff top sheets	3" "
Peak downhauls	2" "
Jib "	2¼" "
Peak jigs	2" "
Flying jib sheets	3" "
Jib top sheets	2¾" "
Jib and forestaysail sheets	2¾" "
" " " lifts	3" "

Block List

Location		Number req'd	No. of sheaves	Size	Kind	
Peak halyard	masthead	8	2	16"	Met bushed	Shackles.
" "	"	4	1	16"	" "	"
" "	on gaff	16	1	16"	" "	St'd eyes
Peak purchases		4	2	7"	Pat bushing	Round eye and rope thimble
" "		4	1	7"	" "	Sister hooks and beckets
Throat halyards		4	3	16"	Met bushed	Loose hooks and beckets
" "		4	3	16"	" "	" " " "
(fore?) staysail halyards		2	2	10"	Pat bushing	Sister hooks
" " "		2	1	10"	" "	" " and beckets
Flying jib halyards		2	1	9"	" "	" " and becket on one
Jib topsail		2	1	8"	" "	" " " " " "
Gaff topsail		4	2	8"	" "	Stiff hook with mortise
" "		4	1	8"	" "	" " " "
Fore, main, and mizzen boom lifts		6	2	8"	Com bushing	Heavy sister hooks
" " " " " "		6	1	8"	" "	Round eye, wire thimbles and becket
Spanker boom lifts		2	2	10"	" "	Shackles and becket
" " "		2	2	10"	" "	Round eye and wire thimbles
Boom tackles		4	2	10"	" "	Heavy mortises, single hooks
" "		4	1	10"	" "	" " , single hooks and becket
Crotch tackles		4	1	8"	" "	Single hooks and becket on two
Gaff topsail and staysail clew lines		20	1	6"	Pat bushings	Round eye
Downhaul (peak?)		4	1	7"	" "	" "
Boat fall		2	3	7"	" "	Swivel jaws
" "		2	2	9"	" "	Loose swivel hooks
(jib and staysail?) boom lifts		2	1	6"	" "	Sister hooks and beckets
" " " " "		2	1	6"	" "	Round eye and wire thimbles
Deck tackles		2	2	8"	" "	Loose hook
" "		2	1	8"	" "	" " and beckets
Reef tackles		1	3	8"	" "	sister hook
(— — —?) and peak halyards		6	1	12"	Met bushed	Swivel jaws
Cargo purchase		2	2	16"	" "	Loose hooks
" "		4	1	16"	" "	" " and beckets
Fore staysail and jib sheets		2	2	8"	Comm bushing	Heavy sister hooks Becket on one
" " " " "		2	1	8"	" "	" " " " " "
Flying jib sheet		2	1	8"	" "	Round lignum vitae. Round eye and wire thimbles
Jib topsail sheets		2	1	7"	" "	" " " " " " rope "
Gaff topsail sheet		4	1	9"	" "	Heavy sister hooks
" " " chocks		4	patent			
Gaff topsail sheet chains and patent hooks		4	sets ¾"			
Fore, main, mizzen sheets		6	2	14"	Met bushed	Heavy mortise cross bolted shackles and beckets
Spanker sheets		2	3	15"	" "	" " " " " " "
" "		2	2	15	" "	Shackles and beckets on two
Deck leaders for sheets		7	-	5"	Single score 2" hole Lignum Vitae bullseyes	
Anchor purchase		1	3	15"	Met bushed	Heavy mortise cross bolted Shackle on one
" "		1	2	15"	Met bushed	Single
Topmast staysail halyards		6	1	7"	Pat bushing	Sister hooks and beckets on three
Topmast staysail downhaul		3	-	6"	" "	Round eye
Staysail tripping lines		6	1	5"	" "	" "
Snatch block		2	1	6"	Met bushing	
" "		2	1	8"		
" "		2	1	10"		

Bullseyes, Turnbuckles, and Misc. Rigging Outfit

66 mast hoops, 28" inside dia. lower masts
22 " " 29" " " foremast
39 " " 18" " " topmasts
13 " " 20" " " foretopmast

2-6" bullseyes, lignum vitae, 2½" hole, jibstay chains, double scored for iron strap
1-5" " " " 2" hole, flying jib stay, " " " " "
1-4½" " " " 1¾" hole, Jib topmast stay, " " " " "
1-4" " " " 1½" hole, Topmast stay, " " " " "
1-3" " " " 1¼" " " " " " " " "
6-4" " " " 1¼" " " " " " " " "
4-4" " " " 1½" " peak downhaul " " " " "

12-2 hole leading trucks, lignum vitae
12-1 hole " " " "

6 bulls eyes, lignum vitae, 1¾" hole, deck leaders for jib stay
8 patent crosstree leaders for peak halyards
4-5" bullseyes, lignum vitae, for jib outhaul
20-5" galv iron stay hooks, forestaysail
30-5" " " " " , jib
40-3¾" " " " " , flying jib
45-3¼" " " " " , jib topsail
60-2½" " " " " , topmast staysail

8-1⅞" turnbuckles, fore shrouds
24-1¾" turnbuckles – main, mizzen and spanker shrouds
8-1¼" " – topmast backstays
2-1⅞" " – bobstays
2-1¾" " – bowsprit shrouds
2-1½" " – back ropes
4-1¼" " – jibboom guys
2-1¾" " – preventer masthead stays

Bobstays – 1¼" tested crane chain
Bowsprit shrouds – 1" tested crane chain
Jibstay chains – 1¼" " " "
Cat stopper – ¾" " " "
Shank painter – ⅝" " " "
Back ropes – ¾" " " "
Martingale jumpers – ⅝" " " "
Cat pendant – ¾" " " "

H Ship's boats

H1 MOTOR YAWL BOAT ON STERN
DAVITS (no scale)
1   Boat falls (tackle)
2   Strongback
3   Yawl boat
4   Chock rail
5   Main rail/poop coverboard
6   Fashion piece
7   Fly rail
8   Deck brace
9   Rail stanchion
10 Davit
11 Yawl boat gripe (lashing)
12 Davie plank

'Names of things were often different in one area than another, but an experienced sailor soon understood that a "yawl boat", in Maine, might be a "stern boat" to a Lunenburger. I sailed with one bosun who called a "tayckle" a "tattle". We knew what they were talking about.' (*Capt. Biff Bowker, private correspondence*)

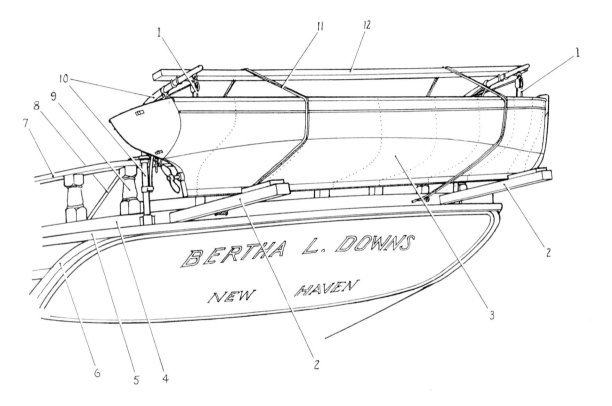

BERTHA L. DOWNS

NEW HAVEN

H1

H Ship's boats

H2   LINES PLAN OF MOTOR YAWL
        BOAT (scale ¼ inch = 1 foot)

H2/1   Sheer and profile plan
H2/2   Half breadth plan

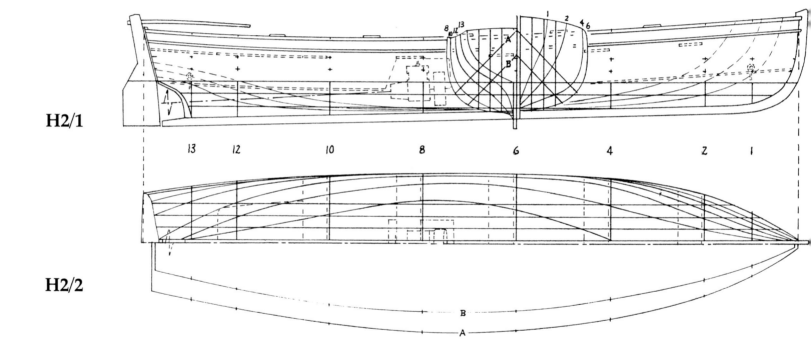

H2/1

H2/2